Corporate
Aikido

乾

Corporate Aikido

Unleash the Potential within Your Company to Neutralize Competition and Seize Growth

ROBERT PINO

McGraw-Hill

New York   San Francisco   Washington, D.C.
Auckland   Bogotá   Caracas   Lisbon   London
Madrid   Mexico City   Milan   Montreal   New Delhi
San Juan   Singapore   Sydney   Tokyo   Toronto

McGraw-Hill

A Division of The **McGraw·Hill** Companies

Copyright © 1999 by The McGraw-Hill Companies, Inc. All rights reserved. Printed in the United States of America. Except as permitted under the United States Copyright Act of 1976, no part of this publication may be reproduced or distributed in any form or by any means, or stored in a data base or retrieval system, without the prior written permission of the publisher.

1 2 3 4 5 6 7 8 9 0 AGM/AGM 9 0 3 2 1 0 9 8

ISBN 0-07-050240-4

The sponsoring editor for this book was Mary Glenn, the editing supervisor was Scott Amerman, and the production supervisor was Sherri Souffrance. The book designer was Jaclyn J. Boone. It was set in Veljovic Book by McGraw-Hill's Professional Book Group composition unit at Hightstown, NJ.

Printed and bound by Quebecor/Martinsburg..

McGraw-Hill books are available at special quantity discounts to use as premiums and sales promotions, or for use in corporate training programs. For more information, please write to the Director of Special Sales, McGraw-Hill, 11 West 19th Street, New York, NY 10011. Or contact your local bookstore.

This book is printed on recycled, acid-free paper containing a minimum of 50% recycled, de-inked paper

To Astrid,
Maarten, Frédérique, and Marc—
Our ki *has infinite possibilities*

To you

Contents

Preface

ONLY THOSE WHO DO NOT ALLOW THEIR ENVIRONMENTS to control them are intrinsically masters. In theory and practice most business and marketing strategies are formulated using the competition (besides the consumer) as a primary point of interest. As a result, other important motivating powers and environmental variables are sometimes ignored. There is no balance and, with a focus that is too one-sided, the entrepreneur will achieve fewer good results in the long term.

"Marketing is war" is a much-used phrase in management literature and practice. It is based on the idea that there are competitors that have to be eliminated. Is this really so? In its own way, competition has a function: it stimulates companies to grow further, to launch new products, to try out new technologies, and to create breakthroughs in the market. "Marketing is war" also implies that one party has to lose. But there is a useful alternative. Making your competitor's strengths redundant is a much more fundamental solution, one that leads to a mentality concerned not with destroying, but with surpassing. This is a more ethical attitude, demonstrating that your company thrives on its inner strength. It leads to better results.

Doing business is not the same as waging war. A bold assertion, perhaps. The ancient Japanese martial art aikido incorporates much philosophy and wisdom which can be applied directly to modern strategy formulation and management thinking. Aikido, also known as the "gentleman's fighting art," provided me with the insight that accumulated experience, continuous improvement, and the way toward the balance of Spirit, Mind, and Body can make a valuable contribution to obtaining powers of awareness, insight, and (emotional) rest. At the Chicago Aikido Academy of aikido *sensei* Miguel A. Gallardo (*sensei* is "master") and in the dojo in Rotterdam of aikibudo-*sensei* Dick van deer Meer I am learning the art of aikido and aikibudo. During the training, the background and aim of the defences of this martial art are explained. What makes aikido so fascinating is that, on the one hand, its versatility offers an adequate answer to any kind of attack, while on the other hand, it takes many years of training to acquire the precision needed to execute the defence.

The word *aikido means* "method or way (*do*) for the coordination or harmony (*ai*) of mental energy or spirit (*ki*)." Aikido was developed by master Morihei Ueshiba (1883–1963). In this defensive martial art he combined ancient combat arts like jujitsu and sword fighting with religious and philosophical studies, such as (Zen) Buddhism. At the same time the laws of physics are recognizable and aikido makes convenient use of the strength of the attacker. Ueshiba stated, in 1925, that he had created the defensive art with the highest ethical norms, using the philosophical backgrounds of martial arts and ethics (Westbrook and Ratti, 1970).

An aikido-based strategy means the application of aikido principles to general and strategic management. Consciously and subconsciously I have used these principles and backgrounds regularly in formulating strategies for my clients at Robert Pino & Company, Strategy Consultants, and during personal coaching sessions with top executives at the Robert Pino Center for Growth.

The differentiating capacity of Robert Pino & Company is in its entrepreneurial method of formulating strategies whereby the client company can strengthen its position intrinsically and in the long term, and in the careful implementation of these strategies. For these complex assignments we have never considered a strategy which directly attacks the competitor or in which the organization tries to destroy a competitor by attacking his or her weaker points. Making the strengths of the competitor redundant turned out to be a much more effective and lasting strategy. This enabled our clients to change the rules of the game and to utilize fully and extend the intrinsic strengths of their organizations. From this (mental) point of view assignments were carried out in Europe, the United States, and the Far East, with tangible and successful market results. I am convinced that the principles of aikido can be applied in business and marketing strategy. Beyong a doubt, these principles and practical examples, which serve as a bridge to management thinking, will stimulate a less traditional view of business and marketing strategy. The examples clearly illustrate aikido principles in business life. They are meant to make you think about ways of viewing, judging, and solving management problems. The organizations used as examples are, in the aspects they have in common, unconsciously capable of applying the aikido principles. Aikido provides valuable ideas that are instructive and well worth using.

I hope you will be stimulated to learn more about this martial art and will further deepen its application in daily life, both private and business. I recommend readers who have become interested in aikido to acquaint themselves with Westbrook and Ratti's (1970) book *Aikido and the Dynamic Sphere.* This reference book inspired me to use aikido as a metaphor for management strategy. In Corporate Aikido the aikido principles are applied and developed into a new concept in business and marketing strategy. For some readers the book will be as clear as can be; others might find the different philosophies too difficult. Every management philosophy has its supporters and opponents. May the principles of aikido, applied in business strategy, enter business life for those managers who recognize their meaning. I have experienced how valuable they are. If this book can contribute to the dissemination of this "discipline of coordination" between Spirit, Mind, and Body in management thinking, the merits for this should be attributed to yourself and your ability to apply the principles.

Writing a book is a tremendous experience. During this process ideas and remarks from others are essential. Naming everyone with whom I have exchanged thoughts and ideas in the last few years is almost impossible. Clients, friends, family, and colleagues at Robert Pino & Company, business relations and the people at McGraw-Hill—I am grateful to them all for offering their comments and thoughts. I thank the people who crossed my path during the past months and helped me to deepen my understanding about life and *ki*. I thank my wife Astrid and our three children Maarten, Frédérique, and Marc for their energy, support, and understanding.

Robert Pino

Introduction

What Is Aikido?

Winning without Fighting:
The "Discipline of Coordination"

Perseverance is beneficial.
—Confucius

HOW CAN YOUR COMPANY REALIZE ITS GOALS IN A manner which uses its resources and qualities as efficiently as possible? How can your organization even surpass these goals? How can you be more successful than your competitor? Management theories are focused on realizing various goals, which are ultimately concerned with two elements: how to increase our company's profitability and how to prolong its life cycle. Many organizations, however, have to deal with variable results and with a profit that is less than average. The average life span of large industrial companies is shorter than the life expectancy of a human being (Senge 1990; De Geus 1997). Why is this? Do we allow ourselves to be led too much by the competition, or do we have an insufficient knowledge of the market? Sadly for some companies, both statements are true.

In the June 26, 1996, issue of *USA Today* there was an open letter from Richard Branson of Virgin Atlantic, the chairman of the Virgin Group, who never eschews competition and has managed to define his strategic levels of freedom in every market (Fig. 1). In his letter he denounced the alliance formed between American Airlines and British Airways. He criticized the claims of the chairmen of both these companies that the consumer would benefit from the collaboration. Branson pleaded for more competition and pointed out the danger of activities limiting competition. He called for the application of American antitrust laws. The more competition, the better, he claimed. I agree with this. Competition stimulates progress, allows organizations to choose, and gives them the space for continuous improvement. The real master does not fear competition. If a manager is afraid of it, the problem lies not with the competition but with himself.

• Figure 1

An open letter from Richard Branson,

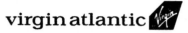

There's a lot of talk going on about the proposed alliance between American Airlines and British Airways. These airlines claim it will benefit the consumer. Don't be fooled. Just take a look at what the CEO of American Airlines, Robert Crandall, once had to say about lower prices in a phone conversation to the boss of another (now defunct) US airline . . .

> **ROBERT CRANDALL:** Yes, I have a suggestion for you. Raise your goddamn fares twenty percent. I'll raise mine the next morning.
>
> HOWARD PUTNAM: Robert, we ...
>
> ROBERT CRANDALL: You'll make more money and I will too.
>
> HOWARD PUTNAM: We can't talk about pricing.
>
> ROBERT CRANDALL: Oh bull****, Howard. We can talk about any goddamn thing we want to talk about.*

What's frightening is the fact that this was said by one of the parties now seeking immunity from US antitrust laws. In fact, the above transcript was used as evidence by the Department of Justice against American Airlines and Mr. Crandall in previous antitrust proceedings.

Mr. Crandall's other partner in this alliance, British Airways, has also been outspoken on the subject of the value of competition. And they also have had antitrust actions brought up against them, one of which is still pending. Robert Ayling, CEO or British Airways, went on the record with this statement when Lufthansa and United Airlines proposed a much smaller alliance than the one he is contemplating . . .

> **ROBERT AYLING:** I'm interested to see how the Justice Department deal with the application . . .
>
> What Lufthansa and United want to do is reduce the level of competition by relaxing the antitrust law . . .
>
> The Justice Department is required to promote competition.**

If Mr. Ayling was so opposed to that alliance, why is British Airways now trying to do a much more wide ranging and anti-competitive deal with American Airlines? Overall, their deal will give them over 60% of the US - UK market. What are antitrust laws for, if not to protect against this kind of monopoly? One would think that the law would be enforced when market dominance becomes a threat, not relaxed.

And where will this proposed alliance leave us? Truth is, the British Airways and American Airlines deal will result in monopolistic domination of North Atlantic routes. History has taught us that less competition means air fares go up and service levels go down. It spells bad news for the transatlantic air traveler. And bad news for free enterprise in general.

Let's put a stop to this deal before the public is left with no choice at all.

Sincerely,

Richard Branson
Chairman

In the aviation business of today it is common to collaborate in order to cut costs. Code sharing, the collective execution of flights under one number, leads to a considerable decrease in competition and limits the consumer's options. Together British Airways and American Airlines handle about 60 percent of the air traffic between England and the United States. The number of airline alliances is increasing. In June 1996, *Airlines Business* counted about 390 and reported a growth of about 40 percent compared with 1995. The only major airline company that has not yet taken part in this development is TWA. The collaboration between British Airways and American Airlines has resulted in an Atlantic network which includes Quantas and Canadian Airlines among others—significantly larger than the collaboration between KLM Royal Dutch Airlines and Northwest.

This raises the following question: Will the big alliances eventually result in four major competitors that will partly or largely pass on the economies of scale to the customer, reduce the average market prices for various routes, and eventually push smaller players out of the market? The competition becomes more intense and the possibilities for competing decrease. One asks oneself whether there is still a place for the smaller, more specialized airline companies.

Competition is essential to keep the industry moving and stimulate new developments, to force companies to expand and develop themselves. Continuous development forms companies that become significant players in their markets and that serve society. However, your freedom to compete is decreasing and therefore you require an even more professional vision. In what ways can you compete so that you may stimulate the growth of your company and make a contribution to society? In practice it turns out that a lot of energy is lost by focusing too much on the competition. If a competitor makes a move, it is necessary to react. Managers have to protect their company, to secure and defend it. Often this defense is carried out with the aim of knocking out the competition at any price. Some management books even speak of a "bare-knuckle fight." Strategic plans are mostly directed at eliminating the competitor. Canon's strategic intention was "Beat Xerox."

How can I make sure that my competitor will not bother me any longer? How can I destroy my competitor?

An aikido-based strategy requires a different mentality. Managers should ask themselves whether it is not better to use the company's resources to realize their strategic intention and to deepen further the core ideology of the company. They can choose to anticipate an attack on the competition and to focus completely on the raison d'être of the organization. A company's reason for being hides infinite possibilities for growth. Starbucks' reason for being was defined by Howard Schultz when he visited Italian coffee bars. He was inspired by the fact that coffee is an integral part of the Italian culture. He had a vision—to change the coffee culture in the United

States—and he succeeded in building a company "cup by cup." This calls for a different mentality. A more all-round manager is not driven on by "force-against-force" competition, but takes over the power and energy of his opponent and gains control of the situation in an honorable manner. This is what is meant by applying the philosophies offered by aikido, a defensive art with the highest ethical norms.

Aikido is often described as a defensive art for gentlemen. This definition is accepted and recognized by almost everyone.

Those who have never practiced martial arts before are usually not able to point out the differences between aikido and other combat sports. Aikido is partly characterized by its important basic motivations, ethical standards, and distinguished style. It is a pure, 100 percent defensive art that can be used against almost any kind of attack, whether this comes from one or more opponents. On a higher level aikido is a method for attaining physical and mental balance. The higher meanings behind aikido are what I call the alignment of Spirit, Mind, and Body. This is what makes it so interesting to apply to the field of business. The organization itself can be seen as the physical component, whereas the mental component is the company's strategy and culture. The Spirit is the company's reason for being, its mission. If these components are balanced, the company is balanced, so forming an intrinsic strength. In the section on *ki* I shall discuss this point in depth. The ultimate goal of the defense is not to destroy the attacker, but to lead or neutralize the opponent. The secret lies in the fact that the opponent's strength is turned against himself. Because of this the defender is able to control and disarm the attacker in a calm and calculated manner. Your opponent is neutralized and will not be seriously injured. Besides the required aikido techniques, the aikido-ka (someone who practices aikido) should also have an ethical approach. In business the attitude toward the competitor is nearly always hostile. But in principle this is not necessary. Believing in your own abilities and striving for an absolute victory (victory over yourself) instead of a relative one (victory over someone else) is much more fundamental in the end. This mental attitude is inherent in the word *aikido: ai* means "harmony" or "coordination"; *ki* means "spirit" or "energy"; and *do* means "way" or "method." Pursuing an ethical motivation (the core values of a business) and a harmonious combination of physical activities (the implementation of the strategy) is important.

The differences between aikido and other martial arts lie in three elements: it is a 100 percent defensive art (in aikido there is no attack whatsoever); there is constant reference to the inner energy, the inner strength or *ki;* and its characteristic strategy is in the form of movements, evasions, and techniques (Westbrook and Ratti 1970). These three elements also form the basis for the translation of aikido principles into the field of strategic management. The practice of aikido is characterized by a smooth and fluent merging of activities and processes. The result is a high degree of coordination, leading to fluent and flexible movements, free from any kind of rigidity or tension.

Even the masters find it very difficult to describe what aikido actually is. Those who practice aikido for the first time usually think that this defensive art would not be much help in a real fight. They have their doubts about its effectiveness. This uncertainty arises from the complexity and difficulty of the defensive techniques. Aspects like anticipation, timing, the correct execution of the movements, encircling, taking over the strength of the opponent and turning this against him, breathing power, and the right holds—aikido is known for its very painful and powerful wrist holds—all require a very high level of concentration. Beginners in this sport have to consider so many things at the same time in order to execute movements correctly that their defense eventually fails through thinking so much. There is only one solution for this: practice makes perfect. Practice is the mother of skills.

Aikido is focused on absolute victory and on the continuous improvement of oneself. Therefore short-term thinking will eventually fail. It is just the same in business. A well-thought-out strategy, the pursuit of improvement of the organization and its activities, anticipation in the market, timing, relaxation in devising and applying the strategy, taking over the competitor's advantage and choosing the right tactics, all these things improve the company's position. Those who look for victory by destroying the opponent are usually disappointed. Making the strength of your opponent redundant and controlling him is more effective. People who think competition is important usually concentrate on relative victory. But it is the *absolute* victory that counts. Having a difficult opponent makes you better in the long run. Competition has two purposes: an absolute and a relative victory. In the end both parties win. In the market there is always competition. Every organization sees the other players in the market as a direct threat to its well-being. But this need not always be the case. Aikido-oriented strategy certainly does not mean that you do not need to take competitors into account. On the contrary, the competition forms an important part of the external environment. But it is never the most important driving force behind the company's activities. The market, together with the organization itself, remains the motivation for the strategy. Only an unprovoked attack by the competitor can disrupt this situation.

Those who find competition important look at aikido from this point of view. This group wants to see tournaments and decide who is the best and strongest. A naïve but frequently asked question is, Can I win a fight with aikido? *Senseis*—an aikido master—find all such questions too simple and superficial. The first characteristic of aikido is the training of the spirit. "If a person without self-discipline wants to show off his physical strength and wants to learn aikido only for the fighting techniques, he will be asked to leave. The only way to learn and understand what aikido is, is to practice it so that the art can be experienced personally," said Koichi Tohei, who was a tenth *dan* aikido master. The *discipline of coordination* will lead you to mastery (Tohei 1981).

Anyone who takes his first class in aikido will be amazed by the fluent and almost acrobatic movements executed by advanced practitioners of the art. At first sight the sport seems quite gentle. But appearances are deceptive. The hand and wrist holds and the direct blows *(atemi)* are so vicious and hard that the opponent is only too happy to let himself be controlled to avoid further pain. Such techniques are intended to neutralize, disarm, and control the opponent. These principles form the central guideline of this book. It is a *philosophy* which complements management thinking.

Main Sources of Inspiration for Aikido

Figure 2 schematically displays the sources grandmaster Ueshiba used for inventing and developing aikido (Westbrook and Ratti 1970). It shows us that Ueshiba combined two important elements: the mental and the physical components.

The mental sources of aikido can be divided into (1) the ethical values of Eastern culture, based on religious and philosophical movements like Shintoism, Confucianism, Taoism, and Buddhism; and (2) ethical values that are more practical and can be directly applied. The latter values are based on the need for a self-defensive action in the event of an unlawful or unfair, direct or indirect, aggressive

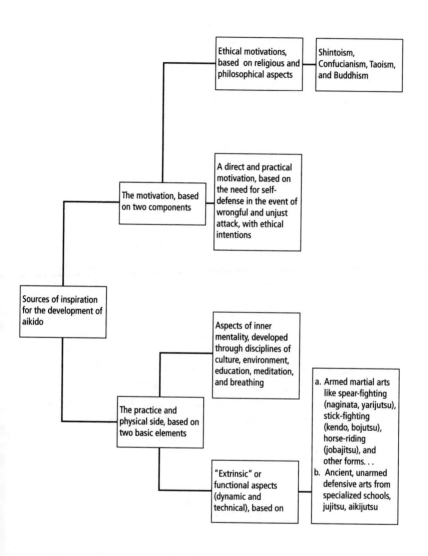

- Figure 2. The main sources of inspiration for the development of aikido (Westbrook and Ratti 1970).

attack. The ethical background of aikido means that the defense is never focused on seriously injuring and eliminating the attacker. The object of the Corporate Aikido strategy is to neutralize and control the opponent, and to cut him out in such a way that he still remains in business. There has to be competition, and activities decreasing this competition have to be executed from an ethical standpoint. The real master is not afraid of competition. He does not fear anything or anyone.

The other basis from which aikido was developed is physical in nature. This physical side of aikido also has an immanent component. First of all, the inner factor is developed through specialized disciplines, learned from the individual's background. Culture, norms, and values are important in this respect. In addition, meditation and breathing techniques are two important factors. In these lies the secret of concentration. Within the extrinsic physical component of aikido elements of different martial art forms—both armed and unarmed—are combined. Ueshiba merged the characteristic defensive elements of these arts with a meditative and religious background.

> *One runs the risk of losing if one wishes to win too much.*
> —Lafontaine, *Le Héron*

The intriguing letter from Richard Branson of Virgin Atlantic combines the appreciation of competition and the attempt to become stronger competitively.

The focus on competition is stimulated by our culture. You can either win or lose. People would rather have "pleasure" than suffer "pain." As a result, winning has become an important goal for our norms and values. In sport, only one can win. One team wins and the other loses. One tennis player wins the match and beats the opponent. Your company has to beat the competitor. All types of sport are focused on victory and the crowning of champions. This is embedded in our culture and civilization. Aikido, however, is not a competitive sport and refuses to become one. From the viewpoint of aikido, matches and tournaments are egoistic events in which one has to measure one's strength against that of someone else. This can lead to disregard of others. Everyone wants to be seen as a winner. There is nothing wrong with this, but self-improvement is a more valuable experience. Running is a sport which allows us to experience absolute victory. Recording a better track time than in the previous run gives enormous satisfaction. Sports that stimulate competition do this to measure technical improvement. This is also an ethical attitude. Winning becomes a measure for showing one's improvement. The purpose of aikido is to improve humankind (Tohei 1966). This goal of continuous perfection is a state of mind that will appear regularly throughout this book. Winning will be given a deeper meaning.

An ancient warrior code shows us three ways of winning (Ueshiba 1984):

1. Winning after fighting

2. Fighting after winning
3. Winning without fighting

Let us see how we can apply these three methods of winning to a practical business case.

Winning without fighting should be preferred. This must be the manager's aim. Because there is no fight, no one can lose. In competition someone has to win. Most people are mentally conditioned to always want to beat someone else. But is it always evident that the other is better? Usually companies want to "benchmark" themselves against the competitor. Who knows if this competitor is really performing better? The competition may seem to be performing better at first sight, but you could improve yourself significantly and be able to rewrite the rules in your market instead of following them simply by looking at other companies *outside* your industry. So it is possible to beat your opponent without a direct attack, by comparing your company with your competitor. If you keep on improving yourself this may lead to an arrogant attitude within the organization. An arrogant organization often loses the will to learn and to improve itself. More than once an underestimated niche player of today has grown to be the market leader of tomorrow. Trying to perfect oneself through fundamental, clever, and creative strategies is "winning without fighting." There are many ways to win without fighting. First, one has to be receptive to the fact that everybody wins. The "winner" of the match wins the match. The "loser" wins because of his new experience. Both parties win in the long run. The original goal of sport was to learn from both victory and defeat. What counts above all is the experience and what you can learn. The best comparison I can make is with running the marathon. Everyone who participates in the marathons in, say, Rotterdam, New York, or London, beats *himself*.

This is the mentality that leads to prosperity. Be open to new ideas! Use this book to the full! Not only in aikido, but in everything you do, you must be eager to learn. Some people can no longer be open to the things they want to learn. They are blocked by their frame of reference from experiencing new things and seeing existing matters in a new light. They judge things only from their own narrow experience; they think that what fits into their little plan is good and what does not fit is bad. But progress does not work that way.

If you take a glass and fill it to the brim with water, you can try to pour more water into it, but the glass will run over and the water will spill out. In the end there will be less water in the glass than at the start. If you drink the water and empty the glass first, there will be room for more water. If your head is filled with all sorts of things, you will be unable to find the rest required to absorb new things. Whatever you try to learn, you will be able to absorb less and less. Being receptive to new things is important and a good way to empty your head (Tohei 1966). It is the same in your organization. New ideas are often perceived as threats and changes, as insecurity. Still, being open to change is the only way to make progress.

Effective Discipline for the Development, Integration, and Utilization of Resources

Nowadays we are confronted with a form of competition that is becoming more and more intense. The competition seems to grow harder and faster, simply because today's markets may well be gone tomorrow. The added value of products, the extras of today, becomes tomorrow's standard. Some even speak of "hypercompetition" (D'Aveni 1995). Most management books and theories preach about eliminating a competitor, or at least "injuring" him seriously in marketing terms. "Marketing is war" is a much-used phrase in management literature. In an aikido-based strategy we abandon the idea of force-against-force mentality. In the end, the mission of every organization or company is to become prosperous. Strategies should be focused on this. Strategic thinking requires a mentality directed at the effective discipline for the development, integration, and utilization of the organization's resources: assets, skills, and competences. "Assets" means the resources that can be bought and sold by the company and evaluated on the balance sheet. Assets are easily copied by the competitor. "Skills" mean the organizational processes which provide value for the customer. This is visible behavior resulting from an educational process; the use of skills leads eventually to improvement and not to deterioration. For "competences" you could use the definition of Hamel and Prahalad (1994). Competences can be seen as intrinsic knowledge, difficult to copy, which leads to value for the customer. I would like to use a

16

broader definition: "the skill, knowledge and accumulated experience (i.e., the expertise) used to execute efficiently and effectively business activities aimed at optimally fulfilling the needs of the market."

It is this discipline of coordination that will merge the company's physical infrastructure (organizational structure), mental sources (strategy, culture, mindset), and Spirit (the company's mission) into a more fully integrated business.

The strongest is not he who has the most
power, but he who perseveres.
—Marc Monnier

The difference between the aikido-based strategy and current strategic ideas and concepts lies in the essential motivations and characteristic effects. These are, according to Westbrook and Ratti (1970):

1. *Reflexive and defensive*

The aikido-based strategy is fully reflexive and aimed at defense against an unprovoked attack by the competitor. There is no attack in an aikido-based strategy. Instead of attacking the competition on its weaker points, an aikido-based strategy is focused on making the strengths of the opponent redundant. Compare this principle to a tennis match, a comparison borrowed from D'Aveni (1995). It is tempting to attack your opponent on the backhand if this is his weaker side. The attack on the backhand may ensure short-term success, but this type of play will also train the weak backhand. Much more effective, but also much more difficult, is to attack the opponent on his or her strong points and make these redundant. Playing a difficult ball to the forehand at the net, makes it impossible for your opponent to use the forehand effectively and to revert to the backhand. This action is more effective.

There are similar examples of this principle in business. Dell Computer is one of the fastest growing companies in the United States; it is a major player in the sale of computer systems, one of the 10 biggest computer manufacturers. At the age of 19, medical student Michael Dell came up with the idea of selling computers by mail. He knew he had no chance of building up an authorized dealer network or large sales organization, as the giants in this market, IBM and Compaq, had done. In 1984, Dell Computer was a fact. Established companies like IBM, Apple, Compaq, and DEC, which had invested a lot in their existing distribution channels, had a hard time keeping track of Dell. This was not because they did not have the means, but because of the danger of causing channel competition with their support (the dealers). It was in the best interests of the dealers to maintain the existing situation. According to Michael Dell, they also underestimated the value of direct marketing. The market turned out to be better educated than everyone thought. The critical success factors worked to the disadvantage of the existing PC competitors when a newcomer managed to change the rules of the game. This fledgling company, which had seemed so insignificant in the beginning, managed to increase its turnover by 60 percent and its profitability by an average of 55 percent in five years. Today, Dell Computer Corporation is now established in more than 130 countries. Michael Dell has more than once been voted "Entrepreneur of the Year" and "CEO of the Year." The Dell Computer Corporation is wholly organized round the principle of direct marketing, and Michael Dell is responsible for the general business strategy and the product development strategy. A new market still to be developed is Asia. The direct-sales principle seems to work anywhere. Competitor Compaq took all sorts of measures designed to control the new competition situation. Reduction of costs, changes in the board of directors, setting ambitious targets, and the standpoint that authorized dealers form one of the various channels for PC sales improved Compaq's market share. Ambitious objectives can be seen as the most important driving force behind the success of an organization. They serve as the motor behind the company's activities. "Wherever the customer wants to buy them" is the Compaq motto.

Aikido-based strategy requires an ethical approach and mentality. A company defends itself, without an attack or provocation, with such discipline and control that the competitor is not seriously or directly harmed. There is also no use in attacking the competitor out of defense, using the same strategy to neutralize the attack or attacker. Often the result is that a company has to look for a new arena in order to be able to remain in the market. Price and quality competition is often a race without a finish line and results in the "survival of the fattest" instead of survival of the fittest. According to the aikido principle, it is better to lead and neutralize the attack of the competitor, and to turn his strength against himself, instead of attacking his weak points in the market. Making his strength redundant is a much more fundamental approach. Creating new values for the customer and standards which are known and recognized by the customer ultimately bring better results. Starbucks created new values for the American consumers when they entered a Starbucks coffee bar. The company gave consumers one of the small pleasures of life. Neutralizing the strength of the competitor can lead to new rules in the market and a higher degree of professionalism. In this way you can work on the company's long-term profitability, its long-term fitness, and realize the aim of creating prosperity.

Aikido-based strategy includes three ethical phases in defense: (1) perception, (2) evaluation, and (3) decision making and reaction (Westbrook and Ratti 1970). These phases are so close to one another that in practice they seem to be one fluent movement. A business strategy based on the aikido principles, merges these three phases.

2. *Center of gravity*

An aikido-based strategy constantly refers to the inner strength of an organization, the *ki*. The *ki* concept will be fully discussed later. The ki is situated at the center of gravity of the organization. As mentioned earlier, the organization can be compared to a human being. A human's inner strength is the result of all sorts of experiences gained in the past, which make up individuality and ultimately come together in the person's character. In addition to their genetic inheritance at birth, people are formed by their upbringing, education, culture, and subculture. The basic character is formed in the first years of life. Experiences gained after that further develop one's character. It is the same, in fact, in business. If a company positions itself in a certain way after its foundation, it will be very difficult to change this basic position later. Changing a company's positioning costs a lot of time, effort, and energy, and can only be realized in the long term—and then only if the market allows it. The life cycle of a company forms the business itself and gives it its specific genetic coding, its DNA. The differences and similarities between two companies operating in the same field can only be judged from the outside on the basis of "nominal" values. The "intrinsic" values indicate the companies' true worth. It will become clear that these two companies are different; they have different ideologies (Collins and Porras 1995), different norms and values, cultures, mentalities, ambitions and inner energies. They have a different *ki*. And the use of the inner strength of a company, the inner energy, the *ki,* distinguishes it from other companies. A company must find its inner strength in order to realize its ultimate objective, and to rise above the idea of winning or losing. It is always focused on the result. We say that the company is goal-oriented. It can only be truly motivated if it is able to realize certain objectives. In addition to the question, How? it is important to ask the question, Why? Setting a goal requires clear vision. This vision in turn consists of two elements: awareness through embracing the whole field that is perceived and concentration. In the end, the vision and objectives of a company drive its economic engine and the way in which it organizes its resources and forms its specific culture.

3. *Displacement and encircling*

Aikido uses a characteristic strategy (movements, displacements, techniques) with the emphasis on evasion. Instinctive reactions, like directly answering a move by a competitor with the same move (price competition, for instance), are replaced by more subtle and refined methods of competition— for example, evading an attack and then leading it in a direction where it can do no harm. In the case of price competition it is subtler to introduce a new brand which has either a lower price or the same price as the product of the competitor; in this way the "main brand" can be protected. A completely different strategy is to introduce a brand in the top segment, which will increase the average market price and make the lower-priced brand look untrustworthy. It goes without saying that both scenarios will have to be tested, to see if they lead to the desired result. So a price attack can be answered in three different ways:

1. A price reduction
2. Introducing a cheaper brand
3. Introducing a more expensive brand

In the diagrams shown in Figure 3, the three options are schematically displayed. In (1) the average market price is lowered. The competitor's action has been neutralized for the moment, but the fight continues. In (2) the price competitor's strength is taken over by the introduction of a cheaper brand, whereby the average market price falls. In both these examples only the variable determining turnover and profitability is used to take on the competition. In (3) the competitor's strength is neutralized and used against him. The average market price stays at least the same or rises slightly, and the credibility of the competitor's price-quality relationship is brought into question. In this way the company neutralizes and leads the attack to its own advantage. The last strategy is an example of encircling the competitor.

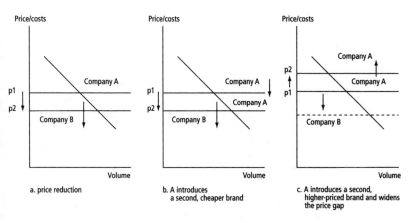

- Figure 3. Three answers to the competitor's price attack.

Reaction to a price competitor is usually in the form of a direct reduction of one's own price, as shown in diagram 1 of Figure 3, or indirectly, as shown in diagram 2. These are examples of force-to-force competition. But reacting to a price competitor does not necessarily mean that your own price has to be reduced in all cases.

By offering added value, the benefits of the total product and of the consumer's total product experience can be increased so that the price gap which has been created can be bridged easily. For instance, a supplier could improve his customer service, or an industrial supplier could decide to take over assembly work. The supply of copier frames with the required optical components for that particular copying machine could give the manufacturer a cost advantage to such an extent that he would be prepared to contract out the subassembly and pay extra for this. In this case the maximum extra payment would be equal to the advantage resulting from the reduction in the integral cost price, while the quality would be maintained or, better still, improved. Or a supplier of a consumer product could improve the logistics as they affect his trading partner. In this way the total costs in the business system of the next link in the chain are reduced, which means more than a "simple" reduction in price. This will have only short-term results. In Figure 3, diagram 3, added value is created by introducing a second brand with a higher price. In this example manufacturer A "encircles" competitor B's price attack.

The strategy of evading and encircling has been used before, and not just in cases of price competition. In 1984, Dell Computers encircled IBM's dealer network and sales organization by selling computers via direct mail. The consumer perceived higher quality against relatively lower costs. Dell Computers followed the strategy of neutralization, as in our example of price competition, with the introduction of a higher-priced brand.

A company becomes intrinsically stronger if it is focused on neutralizing and controlling the competitor's attack. Following the attack must be done in a supple and fluent manner, and must never be directly opposed to the force of the attack. Blocking a direct attack force-to-force, or interrupting the attack, will destroy the momentum of the aikido-based strategy. "Following" does not mean using force. If we deal with a surprise attack, there is no time to pause. Steps have to be taken directly and instinctively. How you react is determined by the experience and the flexibility or adaptability of your company and your employees. Because of this it is essential to assess correctly the competitor and his actions. A Japanese axiom says: The first requirement for defense is knowing your enemy. The first thing that will have to be assessed is the attack itself and the dynamics of the force that will have to be neutralized. How to obtain this information will be described in Part 1.

Competing in the Next
Millennium

> *Whoever subdues his enemy by force only half*
> *subdues him.*
> —Milton

The traditional approach to competitive strategies leads to an escalation of conflicts which will eventually threaten the profitability of the company or branch of the business. The new Corporate Aikido strategic approach tries to offer insight into a higher level of professionalism, and is aimed not at weaknesses but at making the strengths of the opponent redundant. Because of this the company is forced to apply its energy in a creative manner in order to create breakthroughs. In this way it focuses itself on writing the rules of the game. In this book I will try to give insights into how the balance between Spirit, Mind, and Body can be achieved. In practice it has been proven that the perfect alignment of the mission, the strategy, and the organizational resources creates numerous possibilities for growth. Using the inner strength of the business, or the *ki,* the concentrated energy aimed at controlling the opponent calls for the discipline of coordination.

In the following sections of this book, the concept of aikido will be divided in three parts: *ai,* "harmony," which deals with the balance between external environment and resources, between strategy and implementation; *ki,* "universal life force, intrinsic energy," which deals with the identification and stimulation of the company's inner strength, its Spirit and the importance of the human factor within the organization; *do,* "the way," which examines the direction managers should choose.

Part 1

Ai

The Effect of Competitive Strategies Is Liable to Erosion

TRADITIONAL COMPETITIVE STRATEGIES ARE LIABLE TO erosion. As a strategy, cost leadership is neutralized as soon as the competitor introduces a new technology which significantly reduces the costs or makes the existing production process totally redundant. In those cases we speak of evolution toward a lower cost level. As a competitive strategy, differentiation is just as liable to erosion. Piling up competitive advantages will eventually cause the frame of reference to shift. Today's extras will be standard tomorrow and therefore no longer distinctive. Market demands and preferences change continually and become ever more exacting. This is not a bad thing. It makes an important contribution to the growth of companies and society at large. In recent years there has even been talk of an exponential growth in the changes.

Because of the rapid pace with which changes, improvements, and competitive strategies follow one another, the company's overall performance becomes a decisive factor for both the future and the present. Management has to act according to the situation. By concentrating mainly on traditional competitive strategies, managers have focused too much on the competition's activities and have let the formulation of strategy and the running of the organization hinge too much on this. The result is that companies become too dependent, and it is not unthinkable that one competitor indirectly controls the other from a distance.

In several industries the company's total performance has become more important than the product itself. In more than one company customer service is defined as "all company activities directed at and influencing the market"—from generating orders up to and including the physical delivery of a product or service.

Having a powerful brand is great, but in the end the totality of the business activities enforces the preference by the market. This is experienced by managers in the field of consumer goods, in the provision of services, or in the industrial, business-to-business market.

Your company is "mentally mature" if it is able to anticipate the competitor's behavior and neutralize unprovoked attacks. You gain control of the situation and thereafter can build further toward the realization of your objectives. The strategy should be aimed at turning, leading, neutralizing, and finally controlling the attack. With a mindset open to this, there will be fewer panic reactions and the organization will eventually become firmer and easier to manage.

The danger with familiar concepts from management literature, like competitive advantage and generic strategies, is that they can lead to a static approach toward the competitor. Familiar techniques and analyses lead to predictable strategies. Furthermore, the market does not allow you time to grow and gain experience. "Anyone can see which tactics will win, but no one is able to see the strategy and activities that will result in a great victory" (Sun-Tzu 1991).

Aikido-based strategy shows us that a "do it your own way" strategy is better when there is a balance between mission, strategy, and organization (Spirit, Mind, and Body), than when the traditional form of competing is maintained. In aikido there can be no egoism or heroism. There is no such thing as failure or success; there is only a result, and from it you always grow.

In economics the main focus is on self-interest. This leads ultimately to a country begrudging the success of a competitive nation which is better off. This is not because the more prosperous country is thought to be "wrong" (as would be the case with jealousy, whereby one condemns the other because it does better or has more), but because the poorer country is behind in development and itself should be "condemned." A good example of this fundamental mindset problem is that of two industrialized countries which have both put up trading barriers. In 1996 this was still the case with the United States and Japan. Because there are many more advantages in free trade between countries, both nations would have been better off in the end by opening their borders. But governments often have the idea that if they eliminate the trade barriers, the other country may profit more than they do; as a result, there is a danger that their own economy will be damaged. Again, this risk is a threat, not because the other country is better, but because the home country is less able to grow on its own. Because one country is itself inferior, it "punishes" the other one.

The lasting perception is that, whatever the other country does, the home country will be better off by maintaining trade barriers. Because both countries think this way, they both have an incentive to leave the barriers intact. The end result is not as good as it would be if both countries lifted the barriers. The basic problem is the egoistic standpoint and the actual inferiority of the country's inner strength (in certain sectors). The pursuit of self-interest leads, for both countries, to a poorer result. Focusing on a larger common interest makes the pie bigger before we divide it.

The same can be true for two companies. If two companies are primarily focused on each other's activities, they will both make a competitive attack in the same area. One company follows the other, which causes the other to follow the first again, and so on. Price and quality competition eventually results in many products in the same price-quality band; new technologies or functions will be imitated; raising thresholds works only if the competitor actually respects them (many companies are adept at avoiding thresholds). Competing on the basis of deep pockets will not lead to a structurally defendable advantage (D'Aveni 1995). Smaller companies with more limited financial reserves will attract new capital or start collaborating with other companies.

A force-to-force competitive strategy will eventually lead to a race without a finish. A practical example is provided by Coca-Cola and Pepsi-Cola, arch rivals in the soft-drink industry. The competitive behavior of both organizations in recent years has been very clear: in their communication strategy, neither company has taken refuge behind the message that its own brand is superior to that of the competitor.

These two soft-drink manufacturers were already competitors long before 1900. Until the 1930s both companies seemed to be implementing their own strategies without responding directly to each other's actions. Coca-Cola developed strong networks through bottlers, and when Pepsi set up its own networks and opened a price attack, Coca-Cola did not respond—at least as far as the outside world could see. It kept consistently to its own policy; it continued to expand its network and set up an export business which served about 30 countries.

It was during the global expansion of both manufacturers that the competition really escalated. In the 1950s Pepsi introduced new communication campaigns and new forms of packaging which booked good results. During the 1960s both companies profiled themselves with new products and other soft-drink flavors. Both companies collided and entered the era of "hypercompetition" (D'Aveni 1995). Over the years, Pepsi held the initiative in the field of price-quality competition. In order to keep track, Coca-Cola took the initiative in throwing up thresholds. In recent years Pepsi has broadened its resources in order to be able to compete on price and quality, research and development, and global expansion; through diversification it has developed into a strong company with a good financial base.

Coca-Cola and Pepsi have regarded each other as primary competitors for more than a century now. Since the late 1960s, their competitive struggle seems to have escalated. A couple of years ago Coca-Cola started a force-to-force competition with Pepsi to introduce a sweeter Coke. Fortunately it came back from this strategy and the company followed its own way with its Classic Coke. The soft-drink industry has shown itself to be engaged in a complex competitive battle, which has now gradually spread to the drink industry as a whole. Coca-Cola and Pepsi are not only competing against each other and other soft-drink manufacturers but also against coffee and tea manufacturers, and the dairy industry.

Traditional Competition Can Lead to a "Prisoner's Dilemma"

We are stuck with a dilemma. In the example of the two countries with their trade barriers, and in the example of two companies competing with each other with the same weapons in the same area, the result may be that neither country or company will function optimally. Both sides get less chance to grow, and eventually the common interest is not served. Ignoring the competition is not the right solution. It is not right at all. Competitors and their actions should be observed very carefully; the reaction, however, should not be focused on force-to-force. The basic problem lies in the fact that both sides are constantly trying to take the wind out of each other's sails. Self-interest eventually leads to a poorer result for all parties.

In order to understand this basic problem, there is a model that can be used: the "prisoner's dilemma" (Axelrod 1984). In marketing, this model has been used for two companies and their urge to expand.

In the prisoner's dilemma there are two competitors. Each competitor can choose one of two options: competing using the aikido principle or using force-to-force. Each company has to choose which competitive strategy to follow, without knowing what the other company will do. The common opinion is that a force-to-force strategy will deliver better results than the aikido-based strategy. There is a perceived risk in the aikido strategy, because you do not know if the strategy of the other party in the market will be a success or not. It takes a lot of courage and self-assurance to accept this perceived risk (perceptions will be discussed in detail in Part 2). The dilemma is that if both companies turn to force-to-force competition both will be worse off. The best example is provided by a price war.

The principle of the prisoner's dilemma is illustrated in Figure 4. One company (Company A) is in the row of the matrix and the competitor (Company B) is in the column. Both companies can choose between an aikido-based strategy (the company implements its own strategy and reacts only in the event of an unprovoked attack) and the traditional competitive strategy (force-to-force). These two options create four possible results in the matrix. If both companies adopt the aikido strategy, they will both perform well. For this, both companies are given four points in our matrix. These four points can be seen as the reward for their activities—their growing experience.

If Company A turns to force-to-force competition whereas Company B uses the aikido-based strategy, Company B will assume that the traditional competitive strategy leads to better results (5 against 0 points). Company B does not wish to run this risk, and chooses the force-to-force strategy. If Company A chooses the aikido-based strategy, it assumes it will lose against Company B with the traditional competitive strategy (0 against 5 points).

	Company B (column)	
	Aikido strategy	Traditional strategy
Company A (row) — Aikido strategy	4,4	0,5
Company A (row) — Traditional strategy	5,0	1,1

- Figure 4. The prisoner's dilemma, illustrating risk avoidance and perceptions.

The perceived risks lead to a perceived fear. Because of this both companies will eventually choose short-term competition: force-to-force. Both companies end up in the quadrant where they will eventually achieve the least result and the least growth in experience (1, 1).

Competitive strength comes from mastery in one or more areas of competence. The temptation of the short-term win will ultimately eventually lead to a poorer result in the long term.

From Competition to "Convergence"

How should the game be played then? Imagine you are Company A and you perceive that Company B is following the aikido-based strategy. This means that you could choose between one of the two results in the left column. It is up to you! If you follow the aikido-based strategy your result will be 4 points. Or you could adopt the traditional form of competition, perceiving that you could earn 5 points. If you think that the other party will also use the traditional method of competing, your possible results will be in the second column. You can then choose between 0 or 1 point. You will have a better result with the traditional form of competition, so you choose this option. Whatever strategy your competitor follows, you will assume that you are better off in both cases using the traditional competitive strategy.

Your competitor will make the same assumptions. He will also opt for the traditional method of competing, force-to-force. Eventually you and your competitor will end up in the square on the bottom right, both with only 1 point. This result is obviously less than the 4 points both parties could eventually have gained by following the aikido-based strategy.

Individual rationality and the pursuit of self-interest and ego ultimately lead to a poorer result than was possible for both parties. Do you see the dilemma? Two egoistic companies playing the marketing game will both choose what, for them, is the predominant option: the traditional method of competing. Because of this the result for both will be poorer than if they had followed the aikido-based strategy. Aikido-based strategy can lead to collaboration between two competitors in certain activities, enabling both companies to realize their objective (see Figs. 5 and 6). This is what is meant by going from competition to convergence.

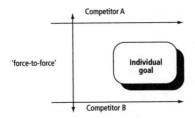

- Figure 5. With the traditional forms of competition both companies miss their goals; the energy is used in the wrong way.

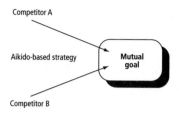

- Figure 6. With the aikido-based strategy there is less force-to-force competition and more "convergence."

A good practical example of *convergence* is supplied by Microsoft and Intel, two companies which used to be rivals before they started collaborating. Anthony Rock, founder of Intel, had already started collaborating with Steve Jobs, the founder of Apple Computers, and Steve Wozniak. Later Microsoft and Intel joined hands and started working the market with their software and chips. After that the world was never the same again. Microsoft and Intel were not competing but converging. They were brought together by a vision and an aim to grow as human beings and as companies. Their competences were used to attain their objectives. Their minds were open to progress.

CNN has a new "convergent." Microsoft and NBC joined forces to attain their objective: the creation of a second news network, MSNBC, which offers a dialogue with Internet users. MSNBC is aimed at a young audience. The new network combines the strengths of two specialists (software and broadcasting), which could well open up opportunities for the further merging of developments.

A recent example of convergence emerged in August 1997, during the Apple MacWorld Expo in Boston, where Apple and Microsoft announced a technical and commercial collaboration. During the congress, Steve Jobs stated that Apple must stop assuming it can only win if Microsoft loses—a revolution in the computer world, as Apple and Microsoft had always been seen as arch rivals. It looks as if this collaboration may start a new revolution in Silicon Valley.

Competing on Two Levels: Functional and Emotional Values

Manufacturers usually compete with their products on two different levels: the product's technical qualities and its emotional values (what the product "does" for the consumer and for the brand). Computer suppliers like Compaq, Apple, and IBM compete on the technical qualities of their products—mega- and gigabytes, user friendliness, processing capacity—in other words, on their basic values. Competition on the technical and physical product stimulates growth in new technologies, making present technologies obsolete. Therefore, competitive strategies should always be dynamic and evolve over time. Pepsi-Cola and Coca-Cola compete mostly on the emotional values of their products. Bang & Olufsen competes on design. Sony competes on design and on the miniaturization and individualization of its products (the Walkman, for instance). Brands like Rolex, Benetton, Four Seasons, and British Airways compete on both the technical qualities and the emotional aspects of their products.

The technical and emotional values of a product are inextricably connected, and are fused by the brand. In Figure 7 these two aspects are depicted in a "value circle," an entity in which both elements interact and are eventually responsible for the perception in the market. The technical product needs a brand and the emotional product urges continuous development of the physical product. They interact. Looking at the two logos in the value circle, Apple and Coca-Cola, our mind automatically provides the products with a certain brand personality. The brand represents the sum of the product's technical and functional aspects, and its image represents the emotional value. More and more the brand is becoming a

- Figure 7. The value circle, with functional and emotional product aspects.

symbol of the company's DNA; it represents a whole world. This is not only true for the brands of manufacturers; the brands of links in a chain can send a signal to the world. Wal-Mart, Albert Heijn, and Marks and Spencer are examples of retail companies which back up the products they sell with their own names. Starbucks competes on these two elements. This company changed the U.S. coffee culture, making Starbucks synonymous with good coffee.

The two elements brought together in the value circle can vary in importance, depending on the market you are in (what is more important to your customers, the function or the emotional world with which they can identify themselves?), the phase the product is in (a new product or one of many comparable products on the market), and the intensity of the competition (are there only a few suppliers or are there a great many, and is the market strongly differentiated?). It goes without saying that both elements in the value circle will keep generating competitive strength. Nevertheless we should ask ourselves if it is still sufficient to distinguish ourselves through them. In a world where things are developing faster every day, the power derived from improvements in functional and emotional values could diminish.

A competitive battle being fought out mainly on functional and emotional elements is the one between Nike and Adidas. In my opinion Nike has employed a strategy which conceals a great many aikido principles. This company has stuck to its policy in a consistent and consequential manner, and not responded directly to Adidas. Nike has managed to make the strength of Adidas redundant. For a very long time Adidas was the market leader for running shoes, until Nike entered this market. At that point, Adidas possibly underestimated the market and Nike's strategy. As market leader, a company runs the risk of becoming arrogant, and unable to assess accurately the market implications of the newcomer's strategy.

Perhaps Adidas did not watch its environment carefully enough. Not only did the market change, but the company was too late in adapting its strategy in order to understand and utilize the changed world. Its information and the interpretation of it probably pointed out too late that an attack by a company like Nike was due. Acquiring the right information for policymaking at the right moment determines the effect of the strategy.

Aikido is based on seeing holistically. In practicing aikido the *aikido-ka* (someone who practices aikido) starts viewing things in a holistic way. You should be focused on observing the whole picture, using your eyes to their maximum capacity, as opposed to observing by focusing on one point only. With the maximum range, your perception will be better and more complete than when you focus on a specific area. Perhaps Adidas did perceive Nike's movement, but it did not *observe* the complete picture of its competitor and the environment.

Phil Knight and his business partner Bill Bowerman developed their first running shoe in 1972, and they decided to start manufacturing it themselves. The production was farmed out to low-wage countries in the Far East, but Knight and Bowerman strictly controlled the quality of the end product themselves. The shoe was named after the goddess of victory in Greek mythology, Nike. At that time, the competition was intense. Nike had to earn a market position next to the three biggest suppliers of athletic shoes: Adidas, Puma, and Tiger. A qualitatively better and distinctive product (the functional component) would be able to earn them a place in the market. Nike also introduced a broad and deep assortment, in order to obtain firm presence right away.

According to the company's annual reports, the 1976 turnover of $15 million had been increased to the level of $6.5 billion by 1996. In some cases delivery times ran up to six months, and this was accepted by the customer. Because of the breadth and depth of its assortment, the Nike brand became known and recognized as the biggest and most complete manufacturer of running shoes. Not only did Nike cover all market segments, but because of its assortment it also managed to utilize all possible distribution channels. Its shoes were sold everywhere, from the traditional warehouses to specialized sports shops. Nike's market size and visibility became an important driving force behind its success. Another factor in Nike's success is its unconditional investment in research and development, supported by a wide range of professional advisers from the world of sport. Nike even developed its own shops, the so-called Athletic Departments, enabling them to monitor the market directly.

A third success factor for Nike is its cunning communication strategy (emotional component). Instead of advertising in newspapers and magazines, the company had professional and successful athletes photographed wearing Nike shoes. Editorial features on famous athletes, announced on the cover of the magazine, had (and still have) more impact on the reader than advertisements more or less hidden in the magazine itself. If this famous personality also happens to be wearing Nikes, this will be a better investment of communication funds than buying a full-page advertisement in a prominent magazine. With the help of sponsoring and the silent guarantees of athletes who wore Nike products, the company hitchhiked on the success of these athletes. In this way Nike indirectly communicated the benefit it represented (emotional component of the value circle).

The strategic space Nike had created for itself was instantly filled by its competitors. But by constantly improving and teaching employees that this continual improvement was essential, Nike succeeded in maintaining its lead in a market dominated for many years by Adidas and Puma. The example of Nike illustrates that this company has been aware of various principles: high quality, segment orientation, use of expert endorsements, and continuous improvement. Furthermore, the company has displayed an important level of consistency and consequentiality in its policymaking. The philosophies of Confucius and Lao-Tse indicate that sticking to your objective and consistency in implementation will lead to better results. Consciously or unconsciously, Nike has done this. The principles of Nike are the core values of the organization. The quest for perfection, for continuous growth, is shown in the Nike commercial "I can." The concept of core values will be further discussed in Part 2.

A Second Value Circle Comes into Focus: Competing in Business Systems and Chains

Competing on functional and emotional value only is no longer sufficient. It is becoming more and more difficult to differentiate oneself only on the basis of these two elements. Until now investing consistently and consequently in product positioning (the emotional component) has still been enough for companies to distinguish themselves. The Marlboro cowboy is the emotional property of the cigarette brand, but equally, for a large group of consumers, Joe Camel has the image of being "tough and independent." What's more, the consumer's frame of reference is changing. The consumer has become used to a fast computer and would like to have one that is even faster. The consumer is educated by the producer and wants more and more products and services delivered faster and faster. The extras of today will be standard tomorrow, and the day after tomorrow they will be out of date. It has become crucial to improve constantly, and to focus on continuous development. From the viewpoint of aikido philosophy, it is important to keep winning over oneself.

An example from the car industry, where the consumer has defined "quality" differently through the years, may illustrate this. In the 1960s, big cars were popular in the United States. Big was synonymous with high quality and status. In the 1970s, cars with economical fuel consumption were popular. Low fuel consumption was considered an important functional feature and cars were bought with this in mind. In the 1980s, smaller cars were more successful in the American market, and today safety is the name of the game (D'Aveni 1994). A product's functional and emotional elements are evaluated differently by the consumer in the course of time. The perceived value changes. Nowadays, big or small cars have to be economical, ecologically friendly, and safe.

In the past, mobile telephones were used because they were absolutely essential—because of the inadequate infrastructure in countries in the Far East, for example (technical element). Another large group of consumers used mobile telephones because of its status (emotional value). Slowly we are reaching the phase where the consumer uses a mobile telephone because of the element of convenience (availability and certainty). Motorola has the strategic ambition of giving each individual a mobile telephone with a personalized telephone number. This also changes the consumer's frame of reference.

In addition to the perceived performance of a product or service (the values and performance of a product in the eyes of the consumer, compared with the competitor's offer), the price and cost level of the manufacturer or supplier are also important competitive weapons. Some manufacturers have a higher cost level than their competitors. This may have many different causes, which will not be discussed in detail here. Generally speaking, these manufacturers can pass on their higher cost price to the market because the consumer is willing to pay a higher price. In this case, the product's price-value ratio is in balance.

Besides competition on the functional and emotional elements of a product or service, there is competition on price. The cost level and the perceived value mentioned earlier are related to this. But in this area too we see a shift. Products are getting cheaper all the time. Consumer electronics provide a good example. Computers and audiovisual equipment have become cheaper and can do more.

This development is taking place in nearly all markets. In their basic service package hotels now offer elements which were considered luxuries several years earlier. Flying to a distant destination is within nearly everyone's reach. In their total service package couriers offer elements which are regarded as standard by the market. The result is that there is more competition (more intense, in any case), that markets are becoming more mature, and that companies have to earn back their investments faster. The product life cycle is shortening and the break-even point has to be reached sooner. This means that we have to focus more on a shifting market, a market with more individual requirements, with niches. Important niches are the germ cells of the mass markets of tomorrow. The consumers' frames of reference are shifting; their demands are becoming higher. Not taking this into account will lead to a downturn.

The current opinion is that everyone has to run along on the same treadmill, and that there are only four areas in which we could or should compete: price and quality, time and know-how, the creation of all sorts of thresholds, and financial resources, the so-called company purse (D'Aveni 1994). These competitive areas will always exist. The danger is that energy may be channeled the wrong way. Who is going to profit if we all compete in the same way? Are there still other degrees of strategic freedom whereby we can grow and make a significant contribution to society?

Strategic Freedom

Strategic freedom can be defined as the space a company has to influence positively its position in relation to its competitors (Pino 1994). An interesting example of a degree of strategic freedom arose in Switzerland. A few years ago, Nestlé introduced its ice tea product, with the brand name Nestea, in the outdoor distribution channel (gas stations, kiosks, schools, etc.). Because it had neither sufficient nor suitable resources for this particular product-market combination, it decided to collaborate with Coca-Cola, actually a direct competitor in the soft-drink market. Collaborating with a direct competitor in order to attain a better result leads to convergence. Nestlé hitchhiked on Coca-Cola's *infrastructure,* and its first degree of strategic freedom lay in using it. Not long after the introduction of Nestea, another degree of strategic freedom was created, because the company had significant visibility in different distribution channels. This visibility made the market and the competition perceive Nestlé as a big player in this particular product-market combination. Nestlé used this *visibility* and the way it was perceived by the market, as a "lever" enabling it to participate in the retail channel.

There is also the example of an industrial supplier which used a degree of strategic freedom. The company (not named for reasons of confidentiality) discovered that components of its machines were being "reordered" by foreign customers to whom no machines had been delivered. It turned out that one of the company's agents was imitating the machines and circumventing the patents. Because this was illegal, the industrial organization was forced to find another agency within weeks, in order to maintain its service to its original clientele. It succeeded and thus neutralized the strengths of its agent without taking direct legal action. The degrees of strategic freedom used by Nestlé and the industrial supplier show that inner strength can be obtained from areas other than technical quality or product brand only. If you focus on the infrastructure which is required to better serve the market, the strengths of your competitors will become more or less redundant.

Make the Strengths of Your Opponent Redundant

At universities and in management literature the case is regularly made for attacking the competitor on his weaker points. In the analysis of competitors' strengths and weaknesses, it is almost automatically assumed that attacking the opponent's weakness is a good strategy. This may be true in the short term, but is much less sure in the long term.

Furthermore, this strategy usually leads to imitation. It is better to focus on new developments, on new and improved products which stimulate the whole industry. Continuous improvement and refinement lead to better results. This not only refers to end products, but to all activities contributing to the company's success in the market.

The infrastructure used alters the nature of the game. This brings us to a second value circle (see Figure 8 at the top of the next page).

The Business System

The activities of the business system form the first degree of freedom. By "business system" I mean the departments handling the company's primary processes (buying, production, logistics, sales and

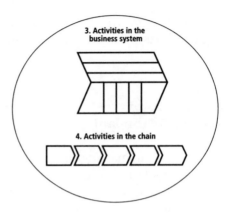

- Figure 8. The value circle of the inner
             competitive strengths: business
             system and industry chain.

marketing), and support departments such as human
resources and research and development. If we stop
seeing a company as this group of separate departments (buying, production, marketing and sales and
logistics) and start regarding it as an entity in which
a series of activities and processes take place, we will
be able to break down the unnatural boundaries
within the organization. A company that thinks
rigidly in terms of departments and functional areas
limits itself in identifying and exploiting its inner
strength. The functional areas and functional organizational structures make it easier to manage different
tasks and responsibilities, but can also encourage
narrowmindedness in the organization. As activities
which can be experienced by the market become
more important for the growth of the company, it is
better to think in terms of activities and processes.

In a process-orientated company people do not think of departments, and they no longer have to answer the question, Did I do my job well today? Instead, they ask themselves if the client got what he asked for, and got it when it was promised. This sounds simple, but it is a radical change for the company and its employees. When a company wants to make a change in this direction it faces a complex and lengthy process called reengineering (Hammer and Champy 1993). Reengineering enables a process-orientated company to use its resources more effectively in order to improve itself. Texas Instruments became a process-orientated company, and in this way was able to shorten its production time from 180 to 30 days. Software development was cut back from 2 years to 8 months. Customer service became a strategic spearhead.

If such a reengineering project, intended to turn department orientation to process orientation, is not started and guided properly, the company will eventually become less flexible, and the role of its employees in the organization will become unclear. The implementation of recommendations will be strongly hampered. About 40 percent of all reengineering projects eventually fail because of this (Hammer and Champy 1993).

In an organization various activities and processes take place that may or may not add value in the eyes of the customer. A customer is interested in a good product for a reasonable price, delivered exactly on time, accompanied by a good after-sales service. The consumer is not interested in the transport company used by the supplier of the product. He is interested only in getting the product on time and undamaged. How the supplier ensures this is of little or no interest. It is important to know exactly which activities are responsible for the added value which is recognized by the market and for which the consumer is prepared to pay a premium price.

The Chain

Because the preference for a certain product is apparently conditioned by technical, functional, and emotional values, and because the space in which one can distinguish oneself on these levels is steadily becoming smaller, activities directed by the company at the market are becoming increasingly important. But the company's competence in research and development and production, for instance, may be frustrated by the inability to market or distribute the product properly. It is becoming increasingly clear that companies are better off if they can distinguish themselves in their capacities and activities throughout the chain

A functional area which has attracted more attention in the last few years is logistics and customer service. These are important elements in the company's business system and activities that run through the whole chain. The activities and players in the chain (for example, between individuals and distribution companies) contribute to the total perception and experience of a product or service. In this area there is an important challenge, but also a potential danger. The chain is as strong as its weakest link. A manufacturer of consumer electronics may have an excellent product and market it brilliantly, but if the logistics are not carried out correctly by a subsequent link in the chain, the company will still be judged on this. In the case of products, services (such as customer service) are becoming more important; in the case of services, consistency in the quality of performance is becoming more important. The chain also offers the possibility of distinguishing oneself with a structural advantage in the long term. The Dell Corporation used its place in the chain as its main competitive weapon (direct selling).

The area in which the company can distinguish itself is becoming more complete; it offers more room for distinctive competence and for companies that want to rewrite the rules instead of following them. Both value circles flow over into each other. The inner strength, acquired by adaptations or utilization of the business system, and by collaboration between successive links in the industrial chain, is a force which is more difficult to imitate. It will take significantly more time and experience to copy it.

By considering both value circles in determining the company's objectives and formulating its strategy, the company will grow intrinsically stronger. The four elements are merged and contribute to the total value proposition of your company. The total value proposition is the total supply which adds extra value to the value for the customers, the value for the stockholders, and the value for the employees.

The value proposition is illustrated in Figure 10 (see page 56). This illustration has also proved to be of use in formulating a strategy for an industrial service company.

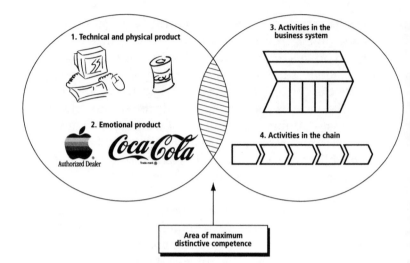

- Figure 9. Where the four elements come together, the maximum distinctive competence is realized.

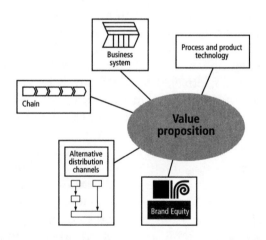

- Figure 10. The value proposition of a company.

Besides the four elements in the value circles (functional product, emotional product, business system, and chain), the figure also displays the R & D and alternative distribution channels.

It is important to add here that implementing a strategy in all these areas could well be too much for the organization. As a result there is the risk of you becoming a master in average implementation. It is better to look at the external environment and (potential) events that may damage the company. You will have to set your priorities. These priorities depend on your company's external environment and its capabilities and qualities. By answering the questions, What makes my industry tick? and What makes my company distinctive? you are able to formulate the strategic options and key issues. In some cases it turns out in practice that the best option and strategy are not yet attainable. This is regrettable, but does not necessarily have to cause a problem. The second best option may already bring the company very far in its strategy. The relevant issues here are mobilizing resources, formulating objectives and followup, and eventually taking action. In practice, the value circles and the value proposition turn out to provide an excellent think tank.

**Integration of Both Value Circles
Makes It Possible to Anchor Oneself**

To conclude this part about striving for a structural distinctive competence, here are two examples of companies that have focused completely on their own values and principles: Starbucks and Swatch.

Howard Schultz, CEO of Starbucks, used four role models when he created the company. He used Nordstrom as a guideline for service, Home Depot as a guideline for managing rapid growth, Microsoft as inspiration for employee ownership, and Ben & Jerry's as a role model for sponsoring. Starbucks started with a clearly defined mission and can be put into the value circles as follows. The physical and technical product is not only the quality coffee and its broad assortment, but also the coffee bar itself. Both are interacting and comprise the customer experience. Its brand, Starbucks, is derived from Moby Dick with all its emotional values, and together with the layout of the coffee bars has achieved a number one ranking in the evoked set of the consumer. Its logo stands for a whole world of experience. At O'Hare airport in Chicago you will even recognize the Starbucks logo on a sign giving you the direction to claim your luggage. The activities of the business system are all completely aligned and tailored to the key buying factors of a customer. Starbucks has its own roasting facilities and sells its products in its own stores. The company wants to stay in control of every process in the business system. Consequently it uses the chain as a competitive advantage, knowing that almost all shops are wholly owned. Additionally, in every store the employees—or partners, as they are called by the company—are trained to pour their heart into it, cup by cup, without losing the quick service. Merging the four elements of the value circles gave them maximum differentiation and a really distinctive competence.

A few years ago Swatch managed to stun the watch industry with its apparently self-willed strategy—a strategy based on the company's own values, the right vision, functional and emotional values, a suitably adapted and developed business system, and proper use of the chain.

Nicolas G. Hayek, together with his employees in the Swiss Corporation for Microelectronics and Watchmaking (SMH), has provided one of the best examples of an aikido-based strategy. In 1983 he created SMH out of the merger of two companies running at a loss: SSIH, manufacturer of the Omega watch brand, and USUAG, manufacturer of the Longine watch brand, among others. At that time a loss was announced of 175 million Swiss francs on a turnover of 1.5 billion Sfr. In those days SSIH had no discipline and strategy. USUAG was competent in the production of components for the whole Swiss watch industry, but it actually consisted of 100 different companies, each with its own infrastructure, marketing, research and development, etc.

Thirteen years later SMH managed to double its turnover and turn its loss into a positive result, by the factor of 5. Hayek and his employees were able to multiply the stock value fifteenfold! This goes beyond a mere turnaround.

In the aikido-based strategy we apply the principles which allow the company to grow in experience and results. Good figures, like share price and performance measurements, are fine, but the value for the customer is a much more important criterion, together with the company's value to its employees. If the last two are right, good figures are a natural consequence. In the end, the value created by the company is its accumulated experience in securing and stimulating its progress.

The case of SMH, better known as Swatch, goes beyond a turnaround and the creation of value for shareholders. It is an example of philosophy and strategic thinking. It fits in with the mindset of Corporate Aikido.

The ideas and mentality of Hayek and his Swatch company are for the most part out of line with established management theories. There is the accepted notion, for instance, that many of a company's activities, such as buying and production, could better be done in low-wage countries than in the company's home country. Nowadays many companies are spreading their activities all over the world. Swatch, however, has adopted a different way of thinking. The company asked itself why Switzerland was more expensive. Because Hayek was not able to change general economic principles and situations, nor the infrastructure of his country, he asked himself how SMH could bring down its cost structure to the level of competitors who had put out their activities to low-wage countries (*Harvard Business Review,* March–April 1993). By engineering Swatch differently and defining precisely the company's activities, he was able to significantly reduce the costs of making watches in Switzerland (Hayek changed the business system).

In the end it proved possible after all to manufacture watches with a good price-quality ratio against the lowest possible costs for a mass market in a country with one of the highest standards of living. In those days, a junior secretary in Switzerland earned more than a senior engineer in Thailand or Malaysia. According to Hayek, the director of a company has to assume that the company can make a qualitatively better product in its home country, against lower costs, than anywhere else in the world. In his view, the direct cost of labor for a watch had to be less than 10 percent of the total cost of the product.

If a company can design a business system in which the direct costs of labor can be brought down to less than 10 percent of the total cost price, it does not matter where the product is manufactured. Nowadays, this component is no longer seen as one through which you can achieve a distinctive competence or, in terms of the aikido philosophy, through which you can neutralize the strengths of the opponent. Be that as it may, Hayek did neutralize the strengths of the low-wage countries.

In past years Swatch continuously asked itself why activities were carried out in the way they were carried out. The why question is not posed often enough in formulating and implementing strategy. By asking itself why, Swatch eventually proved able to realize major and radical innovations in design, automation, production, marketing, and communications. Furthermore, its policy avoided "frustration" of its competences by subsequent links in the chain. By opening up different distribution channels and by providing, through its logistics, the perfect customer service for the intermediate channel, it made its success complete.

Information Feeds Perception and Is the Driving Force behind Action

> *Foreknowledge enables the wise sovereign*
> *and the good general to seize opportunities,*
> *to conquer, and to achieve things which lie*
> *beyond the reach of ordinary mortals.*
> — Sun Tzu, *The Art of War,* 500 B.C.

In the aikido-based strategy it is absolutely essential to make sure you have the *right* information, and to interpret this information correctly. In the quest for structurally distinctive competence in one or more elements of the two value circles, information plays a decisive role.

Not only does information have to be gathered and selected, it also has to be analyzed, evaluated, and distributed in order to fulfill the specific needs of the management. Information should be seen as fuel. The fuel for a car, however, differs from the fuel for an airplane. Information has to be refined into the right information in order to formulate the policy and strategy. Every strategy or adaptation in the strategy needs the right information. This information is also absolutely essential in order to predict the attack of the competitor at an early stage. In this way you can guide the attack and answer with a defense which allows you to control the situation. Foreknowledge is no guarantee of success, but it significantly reduces your risks and increases the chances of success. That is all you can ask for.

The right information enables the company to achieve its objectives in the shortest term possible, in spite of what happens in the external environment. If the external environment suddenly changes, companies with the right information will always have more time than others. Organized, unique information for strategy planning and competitive strategy is called *intelligence*. In the United States this is still seen as an unconditional and essential management tool. In Europe, business intelligence is also being recognized as such more and more. Big companies like Sara Lee, Philips, and Gist-Brocades have had well-oiled intelligence departments for years. Sun-Tzu said, "You can be excused if you are defeated, but never if you are surprised."

Nowadays, information can be obtained everywhere. Internet and public databanks handle more than 80 million publications a day. The ironic thing about this availability is that it is just as hard to run a company with too little information as too much. For obtaining and interpreting the right information, the following five steps will lead to more efficiency and effectiveness in the company's strategy formulation and management (Meyer 1987).

1. *Separate relevant from irrelevant information.*

The difference between failure and success does not lie in how much you know, but in how much you know about things that are relevant. Gathering information in the right way and interpreting it correctly is one of the most difficult tasks of the information analyst. The real skill lies in the right interpretation of what you want to know in order to arrive at the optimal strategy. In a way you will have to have a multidimensional view and determine which questions have to be answered, in order to reach your ultimate goals. This is a difficult process, in which the person responsible must have the commitment of top management.

2. *Gather and monitor your information as efficiently as possible.*

Information can be divided into three different categories. First there is public information. This is information which is available from all sorts of public sources. Then there is protected information which can be obtained by talking to experts in the branch you to know more about. Finally, there is secret information. This cannot be obtained legally. Every manager who tries to obtain this type of information is guilty of a felony. It is immoral and he is acting without integrity. It contradicts all forms of ethics. Specific information needed to determine your strategy can always be gathered from the first two sources.

3. *Make the information specific*
for the deciding authority.

The information analyst, also called the "intelligence manager" in big companies, is experienced in the art of making information specific for the decision to be made by top management—all on condition, of course, that the analyst operates confidentially.

4. *Report efficiently.*

The basic information has to be transformed into readily usable analytical products on which decisions can be made. Reports have to contain not only the right information, free of any kind of interference and presumption, but also the best possible valuation of the information, conclusions, and projections. The analyst is responsible for this. The reports have to be efficient and aimed at results. They also have to be arranged conveniently, and the management has to be able to interpret the relevant information right away; it is thus enabled to take action in those fields which call for action.

5. *Determine which scenarios*
will lead to the right action.

This is your *sensei* (master) speaking. Scenario planning is the best way to observe the information from all sides, and to avoid one fixed interpretation. If you think in scenarios, you will be better able to assess the competitor's attack or an unexpected event. In this way you can anticipate and your frame of reference will be adapted in advance. Perception and the frame of reference are decisive for the eventual interpretation. In aikido-based strategy the art is in keeping one's distance from preconceived attitudes and interpretations based on (probably misleading) experiences from the past. Japanese companies like Mitsubishi, Mitsui, and others know better than anyone that organized information for policymaking is crucial in formulating and interpreting the strategy.

Navigation System

A good intelligence unit is like the company's navigation system. It goes without saying that a perfect navigation system will never be sufficient to direct an aircraft or a ship from one point to another. This can only be done if the pilot or captain indicates the point toward which the company must go. We must have the right coordinates. If the captain and his crew do not know where to go, the best navigation system in the world will be of no help; the system would be useless. If the manager knows his coordinates and has mapped them out, he must also have the nerve to evaluate and accept the right information and the consequences in an impartial manner. The interpretation of information is a combination of personal assessment, experience, perception, and intuition in determining the right action in response to the competitor's attack.

Sadly enough, many companies and organizations work too much with primary competitive information. This focus is too limited. It is best to concentrate on the total environment in which the company operates. Knowing which way the competitor will move may be useful and important, but it is not sufficient. The best Corporate Aikido company will always be the one which has a clear view of the total environment in which its competitors operate. The right information at the right moment will have a positive influence on the perception.

Japanese companies usually formulate their strategy from a holistic point of view (Pino 1994). In the first place, they have a clear view of the environment, its future changes, and the extent to which certain events may influence the position of the company or brand. Consequently, their strategy is worked out in detail. From this point of view a company objective is formulated, a basic objective that is deeply rooted in the company itself. In Western economies, this is called a mission. This mission, however, is often too global and not formulated distinctively. In most cases, missions of Western companies are completely interchangeable if the companies are anonymous. In those cases one can simply fill in a different name and the "mission" applies again. It is better to speak of the core value of the company, of its core ideology (Collins and Porras 1995). From a company's core values, continuous development and constant improvement are pursued. The business system is aimed at creating added value and the organization is task-orientated, process-guided. Increasing the market share is more important than profit. Nobody expects short-term returns. Growth and experience are the guiding factors.

Large companies have formulated their strategy, fact-based, and are on the brink of fundamental decisions. Investment in new technology or a new distribution channel (the Internet, for example) may be very successful, but it can also be a disaster if the environment changes radically and the choice turns out to be wrong. The new central question in management nowadays is, How do I obtain insight into the future? After the reengineering hype, it is now time to develop one's vision and think in terms of Spirit (the mission of a company), Mind (the strategy), and Body (the organization and its resources). Centuries-old wisdom is applied to modern business. This is not a hype, but a reason for being. This holistic view, the core values, and the mentality of the people in the organization are important elements which determine the company's success—an inner strength of the organization which I call the *ki* of your organization.

Part 2
Ki

The Inner Energy, the Inner Strength of the Organization

It's the mind that makes the body rich.
— Shakespeare

AIKIDO IS A COMBINATION OF A GREAT MANY MARTIAL ARTS (*budo*). On the subject of aikido, Morihei Ueshiba has pointed out that a victory in which the opponent is destroyed has no basic ethical standpoint. In the end, force leads to a loss of energy. During the practice of aikido it becomes clear that being relaxed is a much more effective power than the physical force normally used for self-defense. The attacker uses force; the defender uses rest and is prepared to take over the opponent's energy and to use this against him. The eventual goal in aikido is to harmonize Spirit, Mind, and Body. The perfect interplay and balance between these elements is required to obtain the relaxation needed to execute the defense. Of course, this is not easy. It first requires years of training. That is what makes aikido so difficult and so interesting. In the field of business, I would like to translate the principles of Spirit, Mind, and Body as the balance between the mission of the company, its strategy, and its organization with its people. I have experienced that a perfect alignment and even the striving to achieve this alignment creates great power and infinite possibilities for growth. These two elements have to be in perfect balance for the company to be able to improve constantly and to go through learning processes.

The goal of Corporate Aikido is to experience and become aware of *ki*, the inner force of organizations and human beings. According to Ueshiba, *ki* is the perfect balance between mind and body, which expresses itself in the form of breathing power during defense as well as in daily life (Tohei 1966). According to Ueshiba *ki* force is both indestructible and invisible. In practice it can be described as a kind of ingrained natural force which is difficult to explain—a state of awareness which brings with it rest and relativity and which is so strong that it can withstand practically every other force. This inner rest enables people to interpret events openly and to formulate creative and decisive answers aimed at neutralizing an opponent's strength—a creative and fundamental reaction which will be decisive in the market and change the rules of the game. The aikido master does not react to an unprovoked attack—he anticipates it. Even before the opponent can begin his attack, he has already been brought under control—a useful skill for the modern manager who wants to compete in the market of tomorrow.

In aikido *ki* plays a central role. It is the central point in the spiritual way of aikido (Tohei 1966). The concept of *ki* has been described by famous philosophers from ancient China, like Lao-Tse, Chuang-Tse, and Confucius. *Ki* was further developed in Korea and Japan and mixed with Far Eastern philosophies. *Ki* is the inner energy, the creative force. In literature the concept of *ki* has not been properly translated. The aikido-ka describes ki as a state of awareness in which all sorts of questions and events come together and become clear in one way or another. This results in a form of inner rest and calculability. I experienced *ki* during a breakthrough on October 30, 1997, when I was driving on my way home to prepare for my son's birthday party. It is impossible to translate *ki* in Western terms. The closest concepts are soul, ethos, sensitivity, feeling, and intention (Tohei 1966). No Western word, however, can really grasp the concept of *ki* clearly and completely. I will therefore describe it as the inner energy, the inner force of an organization, which arises from the deeper understanding of its reason for being, the totality of accumulated experience, culture, norms, and values, and the interplay between the people and the infrastructure of the organization (infrastructure, rules, machines, resources). Aikido is the power of harmony, of everything that cooperates, and for that reason it is very hard for the competition to imitate it. During an incident in Mongolia in 1924, Morihei Ueshiba was able to defend himself against an attack purely by turning his body around and sharpening his focus. He was in a relaxed and calculating state. He felt intuitively how and when the opponent would attack and in what way he could anticipate this attack (Ueshiba 1984). Nowadays it is something of a paradox to say that the calmer he became, the sharper his ability became to estimate the attack, to anticipate it, and to take out the opponent in an ethical manner. In management people do not usually take the time to analyze the situation thoroughly, to think quietly about their strategy, and to design a fundamental plan contributing to the company's continuous improvement. A study carried out by Hamel and Prahalad (1994) indicates that in the early 1990s managers used only 2.4 percent of their time to think strategically; this means they spent 97.8 percent of their time on operational activities. Of course, these activities are all very useful, but such a small amount of time spent on strategy will not enable the company to prepare itself for the future. Often this time is also used to extrapolate the plans of the previous year. Drawing up the budget and long-term plans is regarded in many companies as a necessary evil and is sometimes seen as "troublesome." In addition, managers rarely take the time to think fundamentally and quietly about how to build a "heritage" for the company. Luckily there is also a noticeable development in which boards of directors and middle management arrange meetings to find out how to compete in the future and how the company should look in 10 or more years' time. This looks like philosophizing, but the companies that do this now will be leaders tomorrow. Asking the question why and adopting a critical attitude toward everything reached so far stimulate the business to redefine itself. Success today is no guarantee of success tomorrow. Companies that are aware of this, stay ahead of their competitors and improve themselves continuously. The more time one takes for this, the sharper one becomes. In Part 1, I have already indicated that obtaining correct and complete information is essential in order to achieve this. In addition, the company's perception will be decisive for its actions and for the reaction to a move by the competition. For this reason a good deal of attention will be paid to the concept of perception in this part of the book.

Leading the Opponent

> *Without the mind, force will collapse under its own strain.*
> — Horace

In *This Is Aikido,* Ueshiba (1963) departed from the principle that the soft controls the hard and that agility vanquishes rigidity. If you are pushed, pull back; if you are pulled, push forward. Applied to the circling movements of aikido this means: Turn outward and move round if you are pushed; move inward with a circular movement if you are pulled. This implies that you react to the opponent with circular motions, always maintaining your center of gravity, so that this becomes a stable axis. Simultaneously this will disturb the opponent's center, causing him to lose his balance and thereafter his strength. He is weakened and can be overpowered quickly. In aikido these circular motions are called *tai-sabbaki,* the movements that turn inward and outward. In this respect aikido can also be explained through the laws of physics. Centrifugal and centripetal forces are able to control contrary forces.

The principle of equality is essential in aikido. Companies mobilize themselves for a fight as soon as the competition shows up. In business, people are used to the principle of answering force with force. If our opponent is big, we want to become big ourselves. If we perceive the opponent to be strong, then we must be strong as well. An attack has to be answered with a force that is at least as strong. But this is wrong. Size has nothing to do with strength. The big television companies laughed at Ted Turner when he first described his idea for CNN. Michael Dell was underestimated. Very often big companies regard themselves as superior and make the fatal error of underestimating the newcomer. Very often they are not able to let go of the past or to question things, and they are not prepared to listen to newcomers in the organization, just because "we have always done it this way." Howard Schultz, CEO of Starbucks, tried to convince the board to adopt the Italian coffee bar concept for the United States. He had to buy the company for $4 million in order to realize his dream.

Another principle of aikido is that the more intensive the attack, the more satisfying it is to answer it. If the force of the competitor is avoided, the opponent has to deal with it himself. Eventually you will control the strength and lead your opponent in the direction you want. Difficult? Yes. Impossible? Absolutely not. It requires creativity and a relaxed frame of mind. Besides, if the company really wants to, it is always possible to realize the strategy and objectives. How to do this is the key question.

In both the actual attack and the defense you will have to bear in mind the real danger. We simply have to anticipate and defend ourselves against the opponent's actions. If we play by the book all the time, the rules will slowly slip away into the subconscious. In this case we may be defeated by our common sense, because it does not allow us to answer the attack (Tohei 1981). In aikido we always think of the different ways in which we can be attacked. We let this sink into our subconscious and in this way we can train ourselves, so that even in the case of a surprise attack we can subconsciously anticipate or react correctly. It is difficult to hold on to the spiritual state of an experience, instead of winning or losing, if we think in terms of competition. Aikido refuses to give in to this and tries to let this martial art function in the real sense of the word. Winning or losing is left to those who are interested in it. The person who chooses for aikido is interested in real victory, in understanding the principle of equality, and he will constantly strive for perfection.

Ki Implies a Basic Mentality of Growth, Improvement, and Deepening

If we do not fully understand the concept of *ki*, it is difficult to translate it in terms of modern management philosophy. The word ki is used to indicate energy. *Ki* connects human energy with the energy of the universe (Tohei 1966). According to aikido both these forces flow into each other. In Buddhism everything has its source. Everything is the result of cause and effect. The idea that coincidence does not exist and that the future changes constantly exists because human beings partly determine the course of the future by their own actions. Everything that has form and content must have an origin, a beginning. In Japanese philosophies, ki has no beginning and no end; it is the continuous here and now. It is a movement which slowly comes together and moves apart again. In Western cultures, birth and death are regarded as the beginning and the end. In Eastern philosophies, however, there is no beginning and end. From the spiritual point of view, nothing ever changes. We have to use all our powers to learn and to create for ourselves the infrastructure which will enable us to carry on learning. This attitude is fundamental in aikido. The learning never stops. Experience is necessary in order to learn. Results are valid: there is no failure or success. Failure and success are so called because there is someone who determines the standard. A company that wanted to enter a new market asked me once if this market was attractive enough, because the average gross margin was about 18 percent. That was the average margin of the players in that industry. But this question cannot be answered in terms of percentages. A company used to gross margin of 35 percent will think that 18 percent is too little, and a company with a gross margin of 10 percent will find it attractive. Furthermore, the 18 percent is determined by the average of the current players, and one cannot be sure if this figure is correct. Perhaps newcomers should concentrate on the question of whether they are able to score a percentage of 50 percent by changing the rules of the game.

Learning constantly, striving for progress and innovation, and utilizing all our strengths seem to be essential in explaining why some principles are so important in aikido. If we want to translate the core of this philosophy into management thinking, the company's management must have a basic mentality aimed at growth, progress, and a deepening of the company's values. This has to result in a mindset which looks further than the manager's career. We are talking about creating a "heritage," the results of which will develop the roots of the organization. The mentality of management should not be aimed at short-term profit reached at the cost of everything and everyone, but at mapping a strategy in which the company is established as an entity, in union with society and progress—an ideal objective, which calls for the mental independence of the manager and employees, especially those in key positions, responsible for communicating the company's mentality and attitude.

Positive and Negative *Ki*

To obtain this energy, all kinds of contrary processes are required. In the East this is represented by the yin-yang symbol (Fig. 11 on page 78).

Yin symbolizes the positive, and yang the negative. Everything has its opposite. If there is light, there is also darkness; if there is heaviness, there is also lightness; if there is depth, there is also height; if there is power, there is also weakness. Everything exists in its own unity but manifests itself in a world of duality.

• Figure 11. The yin-yang symbol.

In aikido we speak of positive and negative energy. The positive energy, or positive *ki*, influences our daily life and actions just as much as the negative *ki*. Positive energy can be regarded as expressive and creative, whereas the negative energy can be seen as destructive. Both kinds of energy are manifest within all human beings and, as indicated in the yin-yang symbol, the positive and negative components are in constant motion.

Having positive or negative energy is a choice people can make themselves. This sounds obvious, but in actual fact we often do not realize that we can make this choice and it is done subconsciously. If we become aware of it, making a choice will no longer be difficult. If we are negative, we can change this if we choose. If somebody wants to be somber, even his posture will be that of someone who is somber. We can also choose to stop being somber. If we change our posture (by walking upright, for example) our minds will adapt to this as well. Positive energy is generated by our body language. If we walk about thinking, "I am going to be ill," we really start feeling worse. Many practical tests have been made on this subject. If you have an assignment at work and you think from the start, "This is not going to work out right," it will actually go wrong, or the result will at least be influenced negatively. If you truly believe in your mental powers, your work, and your capacities, the result will be influenced in a positive manner. Simple, you say? At first sight, yes, but in daily practice things are more complicated. As an individual you will be able to achieve this, but in your organization you will also need your fellow employees to make the positive attitude work in the market.

This philosophy of the positive and negative can be applied to everything. People can interpret one and the same situation or statement negatively and positively. If you ask a group of people individually to describe the image they have of you, each will respond differently, because each person perceives you differently. To put it even more distinctly: The positive attracts the positive and the negative attracts the negative. If you are negative, you will send out negative energy and act negatively, and everything around you will look worse. But if your *ki* is positive, your thoughts, interpretations, and actions will come from a positive mindset, which will influence things positively. It goes without saying that we mean really positive thinking here, not a quasi-positive mentality. If you just act positively, while you are subconsciously negative, there will be no positive result. In Eastern philosophies the human being is the connection between the universe and earth. The energy of the universe constantly flows and interacts.

Therefore, positive and negative energy resonates in the universe and will return in the same way. Positive *ki* will be returned by the universe influencing circumstances positively. Negative *ki* will be returned too. According to Zen Buddhism principles the universe gives back what it receives.

In this situation the subconscious is always stronger than the conscious. In his book *Ki in Daily Life,* Koichi Tohei (1978) gives the remarkable example of a young Zen priest who was given up by his doctors because he suffered from a serious form of tuberculosis. The man had already resigned himself to the idea that he was going to die soon. He figured that if he had to die, he would do so in the Zen position (the position for meditation). Because he could discipline himself to look at his death without actually accepting it, his mental condition improved. While he continued his Zen studies, he healed himself of his tuberculosis and eventually lived to be nearly 80 years old. Tohei (1966) points out that it is essential to realize that our inner strength will conquer disease if body and soul are in perfect harmony. The concept of *ki* has finally entered scientific technology owing to the Chundosunbup Institute. This case is not the only one. It shows that a powerful force can be acquired if you learn and utilize the rules and laws governing the harmonization of body and soul.

How can the balance between body and soul be explained simply? In different books on aikido and in aikido courses, we come across examples which indicate that a state of rest and relaxation is stronger than a state of force. People with children will know very well that babies sleep with their hands clenched like fists. It has been proved that these fists are very difficult to open; the relaxation of the child is stronger than the force of adults. For babies, there is almost no difference between their perception of their environment and the reaction required of them. There is no difference between the mental and physical component. The baby is not aware of your presence (Tohei 1978).

During most of my seminars, my aikido *sensei* and I let business people physically experience the aikido principles, often with remarkable results. It mobilizes the inner energy of the students, and this is of great benefit for the outcome of the seminar.

Here is another illustration: an exercise I learned during my aikido classes. If two people are standing opposite one another, and person A tries to raise his arm with a clenched fist in a straight line while person B tries to stop his arm with force, person A will not succeed in lifting his arm. This example of force to force shows that both persons are actually using their energy to obstruct one another. Person A's attempt to raise his arm is stopped by force, because he is using force. If person A attempts to raise his arm in a relaxed manner, without clenching his fist, he will succeed. Rest means strength. No matter how much force the opponent uses, he will not be able to stop A's relaxed arm. Person A concentrates on the expressive energy flowing out of his body through his fingertips, as it were, into the universe. During one of my seminars I practiced this exercise with 250 people. This enabled managers to experience for themselves how concentration and relaxation could easily withstand the opponent's strength, after they had found out first that the force-to-force method was much more intense and difficult.

Another much demonstrated exercise in the dojo, the practice room of aikido, is that of the unbendable arm. You can also try this to show that a relaxed and concentrated state of mind is stronger than intentionally destructive force. If you concentrate properly and do not use excessive force, you can experience the fact that the body is controlled by the mind. Make sure, however, that the exercise is carried out under guidance and that you yourself are responsible. Once again we demonstrate with two people. Person A spreads his legs a little and stretches out his right or left arm (whichever he pleases) horizontally and slightly upward. At the same time he keeps his fist clenched and visualizes that person B will not be able to bend his arm. Both people use force and if the forces are virtually equal, person B will be able to bend the arm. Both people are tense and are competing. One of them wants to keep his arm outstretched and the other wants to bend it. Both are using intense force to achieve their goals. But person B will win, even if it is only because of his position.

If we carry out the exercise again, however, while person A envisages that his concentrated energy flows from his head to his body, through his arm, and eventually streaming out of his fingers for miles into the universe, it will be impossible to bend the arm as long as he keeps on concentrating. It is important that person A uses no force and keeps pointing his fingers into space. If he loses his concentration, for example, because person B disturbs this or uses his strength in an unexpected pull, the arm will bend. This exercise is not about winning or losing; its purpose is to show that concentration and rest are markedly stronger than force, as in the earlier situation, when person A clenched his fist and tensed his muscles. The mental state of person A and the controlled rest proves that force can be withstood. If this exercise is repeated a number of times, person A will be able to train himself to concentrate so well that person B will no longer be able to bend the arm.

Distraction will make you lose your concentration so that eventually you are no longer consistent. You will lose your *focus*. And by losing your focus, you will eventually allow your opponent to take control of the situation. But if you really want to achieve something and keep focusing on it, the other party will not have its way. Where there is a will, there is a way. In the exercise of the unbendable arm and in the exercise in which you try to raise your arm while the other tries to stop it, it is important to keep your fingers spread and relaxed. The energy has to flow from your fingertips, as it were. If you practice a lot, you can even keep your fingers in any position, as long as you visualize the energy and let it flow out. This mental energy is so powerful that it can eventually represent the *ki*. A person with self-confidence radiates a lot of energy that can be felt by other people. There are people who are noticed by everyone as soon as they enter a room. This positive energy is extremely important in achieving what you want. Negative energy is usually associated with someone who has less self-confidence. This person will eventually achieve less. The mind rules the body and the stance of the body can influence the mind. Both have to be in balance. In aikido we lead the opponent to the place for a throw through our stance and turns of the body, and by focusing on a specific part of the opponent's body. The opponent is thrown away from us or directly brought to the ground and controlled. The size and strength of a person no longer count. The more powerful the attack, the easier it becomes for the defending party. If you can stay calm and quiet but react decisively you will find answers to the most difficult problems.

These principles of *ki* can also be applied in the field of strategic management. Aikido-based strategy is no magic potion, of course. But it provides a completely new outlook on strategy and competition which can play a decisive role in long-term market success. For this, a thorough understanding of *ki* is essential.

Spirit, Mind, and Body: A Perfect Alignment Will Manifest in Breakthroughs

Experiencing *ki* means experiencing the perfect alignment of Spirit, Mind, and Body (Fig. 12). The spirit is the reason for being, the ultimate source of all creation. It is the driving force of activities and

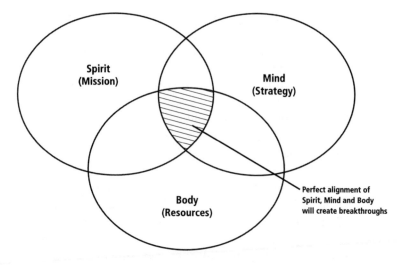

Spirit
(Mission)

Mind
(Strategy)

Body
(Resources)

Perfect alignment of
Spirit, Mind and Body
will create breakthroughs

- Figure 12. Alignment of Spirit, Mind, and Body
  will create breakthroughs.

experiences. It is the connection with the universe
and all its energies. Every company has its own
spirit, which can be seen as the source of everything
that has been created by the company. *Ki* is a company's reason for being; it embraces its norms and
values. It can be defined as the ultimate answer to a
sequence of why questions that is posed by the
management of a company. The why question is
one of the most simple questions imaginable to ask,
yet one of the most difficult to answer. Take a company that is not a soft-drink manufacturer but could
be a supplier of recuperation after sports. It contributes to the comfort and well-being of a person.
The best exercise is to determine the role of your
company in a simple sentence: for instance, "We

develop, produce, and market cosmetics." By answering the why question several times, managers come across the answer to what the role of their company truly is. When other product categories are put into the basic question and when the ultimate answer is the same as determined during the very first exercise, then you have come close to the spirit of the company, its reason for being and its mission.

During a seminar for my own company, we concluded that we did not deliver a consulting product or advice. At first glance we do supply a solution for a management problem. However after asking ourselves the why question several times and analyzing all our activities and assignments, we unanimously concluded that our spirit is "to create growth" and that this mission is found in every aspect and activity of our company. Creating growth is in our heart. I have, together with top and middle management, formulated the spirit of numerous companies with tremendous results. The spirit of the company is the source of the inner creative energy. Every company has a different spirit. Also, the use of the inner strength of a company, the inner energy, distinguishes it from other companies. Therefore, no two companies are alike, even if their results in a certain market are comparable.

Knowing the spirit of your company immediately gives you direction for the strategic choices you have to make. It is crucial to recognize and value the spirit of your company. The reason for being and the mission are important for creating a heritage for the company. Unfortunately, many managers do not have a clear insight and understanding about the real spirit of their company. Moreover, their mission for the business is usually defined as a materialistic objective and top- or bottom-line–oriented. A real mission, however, is spiritual and is the deepened driving force for the whole organization that is impossible to imitate.

Next to the spirit of a company, we can distinguish the mind and the body. The mind is comparable to the company strategy. The human mind has a rational and an emotional part. In business, the mind of the company is the strategy part, including both its rational and emotional elements. The rational element is the quantitative part of the strategy. The customer, competitor, and company analyses, the issue analysis, the options, the numbers, the targets, and the budgets are the rational elements in a business plan. The emotional element touches the intangible items of the strategy: the positioning, the tone of voice in advertising, its house style, brand, culture. In short, the emotional part is the "softer" part of your business plan.

The third element that has to be aligned in order to experience *ki* and to make the inner strength of a company really manifest, is the body. By this I mean the physical infrastructure, the means, the human resources and organizational structure that glue everything together. As with ourselves, if the body is not fit or in good shape, we reduce our potential. Therefore, going on a diet must be seen as a measure to correct an unhealthy lifestyle. The first three letters of the word "diet" already show the potential result if management is too late to correct the company infrastructure. Downsizing and right-sizing are short-term corrective measures that are, unfortunately, sometimes needed and in most cases, not luxury management tools. Prevention is better than correction. The body should be in shape to implement the strategy and to serve the mission. The most difficult task for management is to keep the body fit enough to satisfy the market needs and to realize a healthy bottom line through combining dedication with synergy.

The eventual goal in management should be to balance and to align Spirit, Mind, and Body, or in business terms to harmonize mission, strategy, and resources. In this respect *ki* is the result. It is the inner energy, the creative force. *Ki* is a state of awareness which brings with it rest and relative perception. It is so strong that it can withstand practically every other force. This inner rest enables people to interpret events openly and to formulate creative and decisive answers aimed at neutralizing an opponent's strength. A creative and fundamental reaction will be decisive in the market and change the rules of the game. The master does not react to an unprovoked attack—he anticipates it.

Starbucks' mission is to educate consumers everywhere about fine coffee and to give them a sense of wonder and romance in the midst of their harried lives, according to CEO Howard Schultz. Scott Bedbury, senior vice president of marketing, stated that Starbucks gives people a moment to connect themselves with their soul. After posing the why question several times, we may define Starbucks' mission as "creating a moment of connection to energize people." One of its strategic goals is to become the most recognized and respected coffee seller in the world, to sell packaged coffee beans in every major supermarket nationwide. Its organization is also simply stated from coffee roaster to retailer. The alignment of its mission, its strategy, and its organization gives Starbucks the ability and freedom to realize its dreams. Within 15 years of opening his first coffee bar, Il Giornale, Schultz has since created a respected and very successful international company, with more than 1,400 shops.

Inner Strength Can Be Increased by Combining Synergy and Dedication

If *ki* is, among other things, the energy that drives us to strive continuously for improvement, to remain ahead of the opponent, and to find better ways of serving the customer, it becomes clear that companies are faced with a paradox. How can they be completely devoted to the wishes and demands of the market without raising the cost level unnecessarily? In Part 1, we saw that distinctive competence can be attained in four different areas. Mass customization means adapting product features to unique market demands at the very last moment, realizing scale effects, and serving the market quickly. Won't this put too much pressure on the business system and the chain? Is it possible to combine synergy and dedication? Yes, but only if we see an organization as the sum of different competences and activities which add value for the market and are responsible for the preference for a product or service or for the company itself. In order to lower the company's cost level, activities which add no value to the end result in the eyes of the customer could be taken over by other organizations in the chain, which have built up a good reputation in these fields.

In recent years, many manufacturers in the car industry have decided to outsource certain activities to third parties. This has enabled them to reduce their investments and increase their flexibility. They still carry out key activities, but less important activities (in the eyes of the customer) are put out to specialist companies that can perform them cheaper and better. Activities that are less important for some are key activities for others. This is now a trend in most sectors (Fig. 13).

	1980						1990					
	Fiat	Ford	VW	Renault	Peugeot	GM	Fiat	Ford	VW	Renault	Peugeot	GM
Forge	○	◑	○	○	○	○	●	◕	◕	●	◕	●
Exhaust	◑	○	◑	◑	◑	○	●	●	●	●	●	●
Cold extrusion	○	○	○	○	○	○	●	●	◕	●	●	●
Oil pump	○	○	○	○	◑	○	●	●	◕	●	●	●
Water pump	○	○	○	○	○	○	●	●	◕	●	●	●
Scale	○	○	○	○	○	○	◑	◑	◕	●	●	●
Brake and fuel lines	○	○	○	○	◑	○	●	●	◑	●	●	◕
Clutch	○	◑	●	◑	◑	◑	●	●	●	●	●	●
Pedal assembly	○	○	○	○	○	○	●	●	◕	●	●	●
Steel fuel tank	○	○	○	○	○	○	●	◕	●	●	●	●
Peeling operations	○	●	○	○	◑	○	●	●	●	●	●	◕

○ = In-house production   ◑ = 50% in-house production   ◕ = 25% in-house production   ● = Outsourced

• Figure 13. Trends in contracting out in the car industry. *(Source: A.T. Kearney Study)*

General Motors has decided to start buying in the components for their new Saturn car instead of manufacturing them themselves. This is a major change in General Motors policy. Some components are imported from Mexico, some from Canada. The reason for this is to control the manufacturing costs for a new model. The Saturn is supposed to be the start of sharing resources in Europe and the United States.

Which activities will be appreciated by the customers, and which not, can only be predicted if the company looks into this in detail. The question What makes my industry tick? should be asked over and over again—especially if you want to increase your intrinsic competitive strength with the help of the business system or the industrial chain.

A certain business-to-business company once asked itself this question in connection with an international segmentation problem. Figure 14 (on page 92) illustrates which elements were found by the market to be important and how the different players in the market performed in these areas. Clients were asked to indicate what the market's score would have to be for a supplier to become the best performer. In this way an X ray was made of the different market segments and their demands and preferences.

Besides establishing which performance indicators were important or critical, the client also had to indicate the specific level on which the best performer should be. Indicating, for instance, that "speed of delivery" is important is not specific enough. After

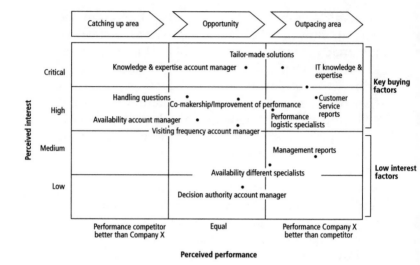

- Figure 14. The performance of a company in the eyes of the customers. *(Source: Robert Pino & Co. Inc.)*

all, what is regarded as fast for one company can be slow for another. So the topic "speed" has to be defined. "Speed of delivery" is assessed on a scale of 48, 36, 24, or 12 hours. The client selects the preferred level; then it can be determined if the supplier is at, above, or below this level. In other words, there can be underservicing or overservicing. By following this procedure for all performance indicators, you will gain insight into the preferences of the market and get a clear view of the competitor's performance.

In the holistic view stimulated by aikido, information like this plays an important role in determining one's strategic and commercial policy. It is certainly worth investing in this type of research. Figure 14 has a performance matrix illustrating some results from this type of survey.

The second step in reaching a structurally distinctive competence by regarding the business system as a unit made up of processes and activities involves translating the research results from the performance matrix to the corresponding processes and activities. In this way you can identify which activities add value and which do not.

When these activities, processes, and skills have been determined, costs are attributed to them using activity-based costing analysis. In this analysis, direct and indirect costs are allocated to different activities. The eventual result offers insight into the roots of the market, indicating which processes and activities have to be performed inside the company itself and which should be put out to companies able to perform them better or cheaper. Both these elements, the performance matrix and the identification of the relevant processes, form an important basis for directing the *ki*, the inner strength of your organization.

Using the method described above, we can split up the competences, skills, and processes in the company into those that generate and keep up the demand and those that are responsible for the supply of products and services throughout the chain. Demand-generating activities are those which, in the eyes of the customers, add value. Demand-fulfilling activities ensure that the products and services flow smoothly through the business system and chain. In Figure 15 this principle is illustrated with the help of the yin-yang symbol.

The demand-generating activities are the front-office activities (activities of the organization perceived and appreciated by the customer). The demand-fulfilling activities are the back-office activities (these are unseen or not noticeable by the customer). Front-office activities lead to dedication and back-office activities provide the synergy. As a result, the business system is ordered differently for each of these. Translating this principle to the industrial chain, we could speak of "front-office" and "back-office" companies. In this case, the industrial chain is ordered differently as well, enabling companies to optimally utilize their primary process.

- Figure 15. Demand-generating and demand-fulfilling processes: dedication and synergy.

In the *Chicago Tribune* of September 16, 1997, Sara Lee Corporation announced that it was starting a three-year plan to dismantle the vertical integration system that it has used for decades. The company wants to be more like Nike or Coca-Cola and turn away from apparel production to focus on marketing and selling. In the article John Bryan stated: "It meets the new model in the global marketplace. It is passé for a company whose mission is [to maintain] leadership positions in branded products to provide all these commodity functions. This restructuring program is aimed at fundamentally reshaping Sara Lee Corp. for the future."

Swatch is a vertically integrated company. The company designs and assembles its watches on its own and produces most of the components independently. According to Hayek, this is the only way to be and stay completely independent. Swatch cannot be broadly represented in the market without a good production system, and without a broad assortment it will not be able to utilize its manufacturing system to the full.

Furthermore, Swatch has been organized in more than 200 profit centers (*Harvard Business Review,* 1993). Because of this, the company is able to formulate suitable and concrete objectives, which have to be fulfilled by everyone. Detailed management reports mean that direction and leadership are very accurate. In addition to the organization of its business units, Swatch has organized itself according to the yin-yang principle. Hayek, more than anyone, acknowledges the fact that activities touching the market are responsible for the way Swatch is perceived in that market. Everything the employees of SMH do sends out a specific message. If everything is combined well and in balance, the company is stable.

Swatch mapped out clearly where it had to provide maximum synergy and scale effects, and to what extent it had to be dedicated to the market. Its production is strongly centralized, but its marketing is completely decentralized. Hayek has not yet gone so far that Swatch could make a fully personalized watch for the individual customer, but this may be only a question of time. Swatch does not see itself as a company which manufactures or sells watches, but rather as a company providing a particular lifestyle and, to some extent, personality. The production facilities are fully responsible for the manufacture and assembly. The watches are standardized as much as possible, the factory machines are fully standardized, and a great deal has been invested in technology, research and development, and market research.

Swatch produces its own chips and in order to obtain scale effects, the company started selling and installing chips in other products, such as hearing aids, pacemakers, and mobile telephones. In this way it managed to attain the scale effects required to reduce the cost price for this part of the watch as much as possible.

The Theory of Attack and Defense

Strength is nothing other than balance.
— Paul Brulat, *Pensées,* 1919

In Corporate Aikido strategy there are two theories. The theory of attack and its underlying factors and the theory of defense and its underlying factors.

The Theory of Attack

The theory of attack consists of two different elements, both part of aikido (Westbrook and Ratti 1970): the inner or mental aspects, known as *ki,* and the exterior, physical aspects. Both elements will be translated here to the business organization. Figure 16 (on page 98) illustrates schematically how they can be applied to companies and the market situation.

The intrinsic or inner side of the attacker is what spurs him on mentally: This is the "spirit" of competition and the company's aggressive intention and commitment to eliminating the competitor. The culture, attitude, norms, and values of a company are deeply rooted within the organization. This is what makes companies fight each other with force. Their energy is directed totally at being sooner, faster, better than the opponent. We see this in extremely competitive markets—companies operating in the fast-moving market of consumer goods, for instance. Tobacco companies (British American Tobacco and R. J. Reynolds), manufacturers in personal care and household products (Procter & Gamble and Unilever) and

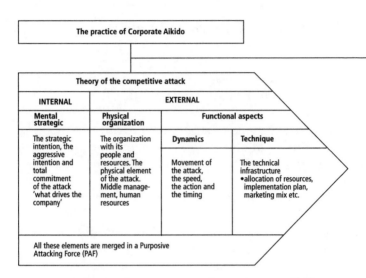

Theory of the competitive attack			
INTERNAL	EXTERNAL		
Mental strategic	Physical organization	Functional aspects	
		Dynamics	Technique
The strategic intention, the aggressive intention and total commitment of the attack 'what drives the company'	The organization with its people and resources. The physical element of the attack. Middle management, human resources	Movement of the attack, the speed, the action and the timing	The technical infrastructure •allocation of resources, implementation plan, marketing mix etc.
All these elements are merged in a Purposive Attacking Force (PAF)			

- Figure 16. The practice of Corporate Aikido.

manufacturers of soft drinks (Pepsi-Cola and Coca-Cola) all belong to this group. However, other industries experience intensified competition or turmoil as a result of new technologies and emerging channels.

In addition to the inner, intrinsic side, there is also the exterior, physical, organizational component. This can be divided into a physical and a functional side. The physical side represents the organization, the physical "weapon" in the attack. Human resources play a very important part here. After all, it is the people in the organization who are, in the end, responsible for the strategy, tactics, and implementation. People form a crucial part of the company's *ki*. This is sometimes forgotten. Formulating the strategy in a management team or in the board room is one thing. But if this strategy is not communicated within the company to such an extent that it is taken over by the people inside the organization, it will never be implemented to its full potential. Two examples of companies that emphasize the human factor are Philips and Starbucks.

Jan Timmer, former CEO of Philips, believed in management that focuses on the chemistry of people and the relations between them. He applied this approach during Operation Centurion. Although his radical reorganizations sometimes made a different impression, Timmer actually regarded the people in Philips as the core value of the organization. According to Timmer this core value has to be protected and strengthened if one wants the creativity required to improve and stimulate things. Cor Boonstra took over his duties and responsibilities in 1996. Boonstra, formerly COO of the Sara Lee Corporation is someone who mobilizes his human resources to put the objective of growth and power into practice. His management style, regarded as tough but fair by the outside world, guided Philips through a second reorganization phase, needed to enable the company to compete in the future. Boonstra's approach, "Let's make things better," pursued the philosophy that Philips must keep improving and that development is an important motor for generating value for customers, employees, and shareholders. This philosophy is in accordance with the values and principles of aikido—balance, coordination, discipline, and neutralization of the strengths of opponents. For Philips, aikido-based strategy implies crystalizing its strategy further.

Starbucks introduced the Bean Stock Plan for its employees, using Microsoft as an inspiration for employee ownership. Starbucks does not speak of employees but of barista or partners. In 1997, Starbucks claimed to have 25,000 partners. According to Schultz, CEO of the company, this stock plan and the way they treat their people is one of the critical factors for Starbucks' tremendous success. Starbucks' annual report states: "We"re not in the coffee business serving people, we are in the people business serving coffee. You are welcome here, as interesting and individual as you are." The company has two recipes. In the first place, they take care of their people, because their employees are responsible for communicating Starbucks' passion for coffee. Secondly, they take care of their customers. Starbucks pays its new employees a salary above entry level and offers health insurance next to the stock options. Even the Clinton administration has praised Starbucks' health care package. Every employee has to go through a training program at Starbucks' coffee school. Partners are educated in coffee knowledge, retailing, brewing the perfect cup, relationship skills, and customer service. The company has been lauded for its progressive business ideals.

The functional component has a dynamic and a technical side. The dynamic side is formed by the movement of the attack; the speed and the action determine the success of the attack. If the execution of a movement lacks action or speed, the eventual result of the attack will be limited. In addition to the speed and dynamics, the technique of the competitor's attack is also a decisive factor in obtaining a competitive advantage. The technical infrastructure used by the organization will determine the result. Attackers focusing on pure strength will be deceived in the end. "Technical infrastructure" means the company's business system (sourcing, internal logistics, production, marketing and sales, and external logistics) and the allocation of resources in supportive functional areas, for example, research and development, marketing and sales budgets, the marketing mix, the use of the media, and collaboration with intermediate channels. For this we refer to the value circles discussed earlier. All these factors together form the purposive attacking force (PAF).

"Purposive attacking force" has two meanings. In the first place the word "attacking" should not be interpreted literally, since there is no attack in aikido. Keeping the ethical background of aikido in mind, it would be better to speak of the purposive *anticipating force.* Anticipating changes in the environment or an unprovoked attack by a competitor means being proactive, thinking ahead, and creating your own future. In this way you will stay in control.

In the second sense of the word, PAF is literally an attacking force, if your competitor really intends to damage or destroy you. To capture both meanings in one term, we shall speak of the purposive attacking force. In this way it will fit in better with contemporary ideas on competing.

PAF is a combination of the strategic intention, the organization and its people, the dynamics of the competitive actions, and the technical infrastructure used by the company. The purposive attacking force (Fig. 17) ensures that the company's strategy implementation is well balanced. If these components are not balanced, the attack will be less successful or miss its goal, and the result will be poor in the long term.

Having a good strategy is worthless if it is not implemented properly. If the company is badly organized, there is no use in implementing a strategic option. Not only the human element is important in this respect, but also the financial side of the organization. Liquidity is an important condition for financing the implementation. The success of the strategy will also depend on the timing and speed of the implementation. Good strategy and organization, combined with poor timing or slow implementation will still lead to poor results.

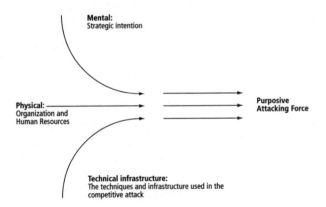

- Figure 17. The purposive attacking force is the fusion of mental and physical elements and the infrastructure.

Introducing fax machines, mobile telephones, agendas, electronic maps, or pocket-size audiovisual devices is possible, but it is only useful if the market is ready. Even if the strategy is right, the organization fit for implementing the strategy, the strategy understood and supported by the people in the company, and the timing and dynamics of the attack correct, the result may still be poor if the infrastructure is not used properly. Your distribution, budget allocation, research and development, advertising, and promotion have to be right. If they are not fully tuned to the other three elements, the attack will miss its ultimate goal.

An example of an attack that was perfectly balanced was the way Honda checkmated Harley Davidson, market leader at the time, in the United States.

Honda introduced their motorcycles in the United States by encircling Harley Davidson. In the 1950s there were a number of major players in the American market: Harley Davidson, the indisputable market leader; Norton and Triumph from Great Britain; and BMW from Germany. Honda's success in penetrating the American market was due to three elements in their marketing strategy (the inner component of the purposive attacking force). Honda focused on a completely different target group, developed a purposive communication strategy around the theme, "You meet the nicest people on a Honda" (technical infrastructure), and introduced the lighter motorcycle to the market (the physical, product, and organizational aspects). At first, Harley Davidson hardly responded to

Honda's invasion. It flattered itself with the idea that it remained the leader in the market for full-size motorcycles, which still had a leather-jacket image. Above all the police had chosen for the Harley Davidson and that was regarded as an important opinion-leading group. But Honda made the market grow significantly. Harley Davidson's market share was put under heavy pressure, although the level of total sales remained reasonably steady. The company made a miscalculation by underestimating Honda. In aikido it is very important that the one attacked anticipates the attack and then takes over and neutralizes it. Harley Davidson did not anticipate, did not react, did not take over Honda's energy, and did not neutralize the attack. Instead, it kept on relying on its imagined superiority. In aikido self-satisfaction is merely a sign that one has not yet attained mastery and the balance between body and soul. Harley Davidson was self-satisfied, did not display intrinsic mastery, although this was suggested by its market share figure, and certainly did not find a balance of strategy, culture, and organization with its people. The management was completely stuck in the past and adopted the attitude that "It always went well, so why change things?" It never asked itself the "why" question. It was sure that no one could beat the company or damage it.

Honda implemented a strategy based on encircling Harley Davidson. It focused on a broad target group with an independent lifestyle who did not want to be associated with the negative image of motorcycling at that time. By making its motorcycles lighter and more user-friendly, by marketing them as a worthy high-quality alternative to the car, and by distributing their products on sites downtown (they even opened a dealership on Madison Avenue in New York), Honda managed to change the motorcycling image. The ingredients of Honda's success lay not only in the right marketing mix (technical infrastructure) and approach (mentality, attitude) to the market. Its mentality and attitude showed it was not afraid of Harley Davidson (the mental component, *ki*). Lots of companies believe they will not be able to capture a piece of the market if there is a dominant player. As a result, many strategies and options are not even investigated. It is only the perception, however, that makes people act like this; the real situation is always filtered and the action or reaction is the result of the perception. If a company understands that its perception is the driving force behind its activities, and that outward show of aggression can be perceived negatively, it will be able to stand back from the situation and try to approach it holistically. An individual interpretation based on facts, creativity, and the will to achieve something will always lead to good results. Honda spotted its degrees of strategic freedom, formulated its strategy, implemented this consistently, and changed the rules of the game.

In the case of Honda and Harley Davidson there was no direct attack. A direct attack is a competitive action aimed at one aspect only—for example, price competition, comparable advertising (communications), an entry strategy carried out in the same market (this was certainly not the case with Honda), or a direct-imitation strategy. Honda used the "circle attack." It defined another primary target group, introduced a product which was clearly different, and used different strategies in distribution and communication. The combination of these three elements (an "emergent" strategy, according to Mintzberg) illustrates how Honda "encircled" Harley Davidson. In Figures 18 and 19 (derived from Westbrook and Ratti) these two attacks are represented visually.

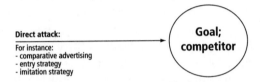

- Figure 18. The direct, traditional competitive attack.

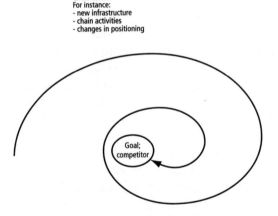

- Figure 19. The circle attack. The company enters the market with a different-mix strategy.

Another example of an encircling strategy is provided by a European industrial company which was not fully utilizing the market potential of an important geographical area, the United States. The company depended for a large part of its turnover on representation in this area. Because of this, it was unable to gain knowledge of the market; the infrastructure, the purchasing and investment behavior of the customers, the market potential, and the profitability were unknown, or were at least unclear. The company decided to gain an important measure of control over this market area. Through an in-depth study of the market, the company became familiar with its dynamics, its potential, and the competition field. It also obtained a clear insight into the external environment and possible events. Through company management good vision was developed and the company's core values could be used as the basis for the strategy and its implementation.

The core values and the *ki* of the company were communicated to a small project group and further deepened. After testing the market and studying different possibilities for serving it, the company drew up an operational infrastructure in order to secure a first result in a relatively easy manner. The company decided to found a small, efficient organization in North America, supported by nine organizations with the same basic values. In this way the organization became a network that was strongly entrepreneurial in order to exploit the significant market share. By using this strategy the company encircled the existing infrastructure, which had proved to be too limited. A noticeable aspect of the strategy formulation and implementation is that the company did not aim primarily at outsmarting the existing competition in this area. With a wholly individual and relaxed policy, with a good overall vision of the market, by using the core values of the organization as a foundation, and by being aware of its *ki*, the company enabled itself to grow very rapidly.

The Theory of Defense

In the theory of defense we can also distinguish a mental and a physical side. In Fig. 20 the theory of defense is illustrated. The components in this figure are equal to those of the competitor (the attacker), but this time with a totally different ethical background. The inner, intrinsic side of the defending company is the center of inner stability and control. This company has a thorough and clear insight into the market, the developments, and the strategic intentions of the competitors. It has a clear and consistently formulated strategy and culture, and its relations, both internal and external, are in full communication with the organization and are carried by it. In other words, the basic values, the company's core ideology, are optimally shared (Collins and Porras 1995). Company examples of this are Hewlett-Packard, 3M, and Walt Disney.

In addition to this well-balanced and consistently strong ideological strategy, the organization with its resources, staff, means, and finances is fully in tune and at one with this strategy. The physical organization is seen as a well-oiled machine which can be utilized optimally as a defensive weapon.

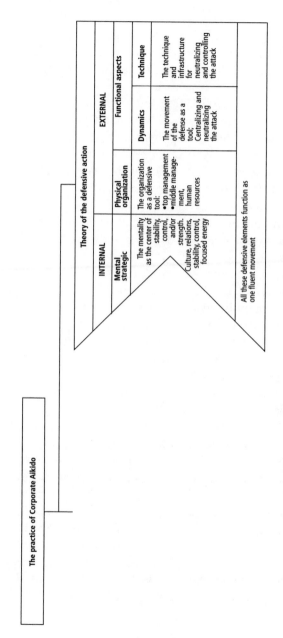

● Figure 20. The practice of Corporate Aikido: defensive elements in a company situation.

The functional elements of the external factors of the defense lie also in the dynamics and timing of the defense and in the company's technical infrastructure (the business system, allocation of budgets, the marketing mix). The dynamics and the timing form the movement of centralization and extension. In aikido the defender takes over the attack. This is a difficult area in understanding and applying the aikido principles in the field of management. It seems unnatural to approach your enemy if he attacks you. The natural reaction would be to ward off the attack and pull back. The essence of aikido is in anticipating and taking over the strength of the opponent—to neutralize *and* control your competitor. For example, when a company introduces a product in the lower region of the market in order to attack the market leader indirectly on price, you can see that the company approaches the enemy by introducing a brand which is priced even higher than that of the existing market leader. By widening the price differential between the brands on the market so much that the product of the "price fighter" becomes unbelievably cheap, the strength of the enemy is broken. The technical infrastructure is the same as that of the competitor, but the defense is directed much more at the business system and the chain infrastructure. As a result, the attack is neutralized in the long term. It is also possible to take over the attack in a relatively short time (by positioning and distribution politics). All these factors are interconnected. The strategy is stable, the organization works as a well-trained unit, the timing of the defense is perfect thanks to the right information, and the techniques are aimed at the functional and emotional components of a product as well as at the company's business system and chain insight and at its market activities. In other words: The company is utilizing the value circles to the max.

The functional combination of the attack and the defense develops the discipline of coordination which is so characteristic for aikido. In Fig. 21 (on page 112) this combination is represented visually. This figure clearly shows that there is no question of direct confrontation between two business systems (force-to-force); instead we see that the strength of the attack is absorbed, led, and controlled according to the aikido principle. In this way it is better for the defending company to "enclose" the point of the attacker. The company adapts itself to its strategy, as it were, and the whole organization goes along with this. An absolute condition is that the company operates as a unit, in which the mission (Spirit), the strategy (the Mind), and the organization with its human resources (the Body) are all in balance.

A Corporate Aikido strategy is not a well-formulated business definition or a master plan aimed at destroying the competition as completely and quickly as possible. It is more concerned with "strategic accommodation," the ability to adapt oneself quickly and directly to the changing environment. A Corporate Aikido strategy implies that there is no such thing as a leader who formulates the strategy and is regarded as the only one who sees the absolute truth. We assume that the strategy is developed by the organization as a whole and that the total inner strength, energy, or *ki* is utilized. The implementation also has to be by the whole

The practice of Corporate Aikido

Theory of the competitive attack

INTERNAL	EXTERNAL		
Mental strategic	Functional aspects		
	Physical organization	Dynamics	Technique
The strategic intention, the aggressive intention and total commitment of the attack "what drives the company"	The organization with its people and resources. The physical element of the attack. Middle management, human resources	Movement of the attack, the speed, the action and the timing	The technical infrastructure •allocation of resources, implementation plan, marketing mix, etc.

All these elements are merged in a Purposive Attacking Force (PAF)

Theory of the defensive action

INTERNAL	EXTERNAL		
Mental strategic	Functional aspects		
	Physical organization	Dynamics	Technique
The mentality as the center of stability, control and/or strength. Culture, relations, stability, control, focused energy	The organization as a defensive tool: •top management •middle management, human resources	The movement of the defense as a tool: Centralizing and neutralizing the attack	The technique and infrastructure for neutralizing and controlling the attack

All these defensive elements function as one fluent movement

- Figure 21. The practice of Corporate Aikido. The attack is taken over and neutralized with an ethical background.

organization. The capacity of the company lies in creating a constant dialogue between middle and top management and in applying the formulated strategy throughout the organization. According to Japanese management, strategy can be defined as the sum of all ideas and activities required to make the organization function successfully as an adaptive mechanism. To achieve this, our perception, our motivating forces, and the effect of our actions are very important.

Perception, Evaluation, and Motivation behind Behavior and Action

In Fig. 20 (page 109) and Fig. 22 (on page 114) we have illustrated the theory of defense. Important for the defense is the way you picture the attack. This view is formed by internal factors. These factors are strongly dependent on the manager's maturity in handling tasks, his or her area of experience, frame of reference, mentality, and stability in behavior. The internal factors are centralization, focus, "encircling," control, and consistency. As discussed earlier, the external factors lie more in the functional area, namely, utilization of the infrastructure, and in the physical component, namely, the organization with its resources which can be used as a defensive instrument.

Each defense takes place in three phases: the perception, the evaluation decision, and the action or reaction (Fig. 23 on page 115). This process usually precedes the attack and sometimes takes place at

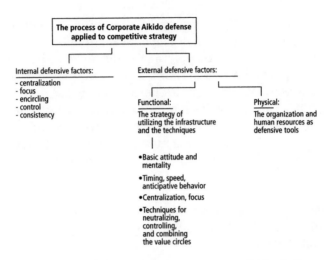

- Figure 22. The process of Corporate Aikido defense applied to competitive strategy.

the same time. Timing plays a decisive role. This makes it necessary for the company to have a good navigation system. Only with the right information at the right moment and place, and with the right interpretation, will the manager be able to go through the process of perception, decision, action swiftly and fluently. With a skilled *aikido-ka* all this happens almost simultaneously. In business the process can be shortened not only by the speed and accuracy of the intelligence, but also by training the organization to think in terms of scenarios. By now many companies are aware that, in addition to having a clever strategy, it is also vital to keep options open if things happen unexpectedly. Not everything can be thought out in advance, but many situations can be simulated.

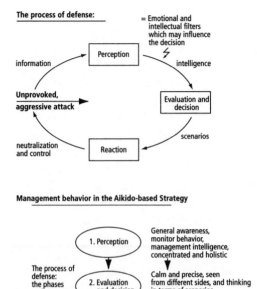

The process of defense:

= Emotional and intellectual filters which may influence the decision

information

Perception

intelligence

Unprovoked, aggressive attack

Evaluation and decision

neutralization and control

Reaction

scenarios

Management behavior in the Aikido-based Strategy

1. Perception

General awareness, monitor behavior, management intelligence, concentrated and holistic

The process of defense: the phases and management qualities

2. Evaluation and decision

Calm and precise, seen from different sides, and thinking in terms of scenarios

3. Anticipation and reaction

-Specific
-Directly
-Decisive
-Consistently

- Figure 23. The process of Corporate Aikido, the phases and qualities.

Scenarios should be evaluated on three fundamental aspects: to what extent do they contribute positively to the growth of the company, the business unit, division or product; what is the added value of the scenario's result for the eventual customer (this may be an intermediate link in the industrial chain or the end user); and to what extent can the scenario make the strength of the competitor redundant or lead, neutralize, and control the competitive attack? By thinking in terms of scenarios, the company's insecurity and assumed risks can be placed in a better perspective; in this way they can be assessed more adequately. Assessing scenarios and working out a number of proactive strategies will involve investment. But the value of the information gained significantly exceeds the cost. Japanese companies like Matsushita investigate scenarios and assess their consequences and the chances of them working out. The Royal Dutch/Shell Group develops scenarios in order to be able to formulate strategies better and to prepare for events that would otherwise be unexpected.

If you learn to think in scenarios, you will be better able to estimate the chance of a competitor attacking, and what the impact will be. Companies that think this way reach a higher level of professionalism in formulating their strategies. They try to gather foreknowledge about their branch and the relevant environmental variables which could influence their worldwide market or competitive position. Managers often believe that scenario thinking does not gain much, because the scenarios are fantasy or only apparent truths. Good scenarios, however, are very important in anticipating certain events. One's frame of reference is adapted in advance and one becomes more alert. Reacting quickly or anticipating becomes easier. Adaptation of the frame of reference is the most important result of thinking in scenarios.

As far as interpretation is concerned, the first phase, perception, will be more successful if there is a general awareness of the unexpected and concentration during observation. You must observe as objectively as possible. Objectivity depends on the degree of impartiality with which you perceive things, and this in itself depends on the extent to which the manager and his team have reached a kind of "mental independence." If you are not able to keep a mental distance between yourself (your company) and the competitor, events will dominate you and you will be unable to regard them from an open and holistic point of view or evaluate them in a relaxed frame of mind.

In the second phase, evaluation and decision, the different elements of the competitor's action are examined and interpreted. What is the strategic intention? What is the competitor's culture (norms and values)? What organizational elements are used in the attack? What infrastructure is used, and which of the four elements in the value circles are utilized?

In the third phase, the action or reaction phase, the decision is implemented. The action should be aimed at leading and neutralizing the competitor's action in order to regain control over the situation.

If an organization is trained in aikido principles, these three phases will proceed very quickly and almost as one. This is the ultimate objective of the aikido philosophy. In aikido there is the basic assumption that these three phases of the process are fluent and that they are more or less started before the competitor's attack. To achieve this, foreknowledge is required (a business intelligence system that functions optimally); furthermore, management must have a very open mindset so that its perception and interpretation can be optimized; finally, the organization has to be well trained and must operate as a coherent unit in which the *ki* is well controlled.

This well-trained, coherent organization can be formed by recognizing values, giving them priorities, communicating them, and living by them. Companies like 3M, American Express, Marriott, Motorola, and Walt Disney are good examples. They all use a priority ladder for values and are consistent in observing them. There is also a core ideology (Collins and Porras 1995). What is crucial here is not so much the values themselves, but rather the company's sincere belief in them and in its degree of consistency. Starbucks will never neglect its values. They form a significant part of the way it operates and are an important ingredient of its mission.

Motorola has a number of deep-rooted values determining the company's course. One of the company's objectives is to provide each consumer with a personal telephone number; in this way a phone number will no longer be tied exclusively to a certain location or group of people. It delivers top-quality products for a reasonable price. The company also tries to utilize the creativity within the organization and strives for continuous improvement. Honesty and integrity are the ethical elements in everything this company aims at. Sony's core value is to adapt its appliances and innovations to the public interest. It tries to make the impossible possible and basic Japanese philosophies are at the center of all its actions. Sony wants to be a pioneer. Walt Disney has a very good feel for detail and consistency. This is clearly demonstrated by the company's statements directed at the market and at employees. It also tries to improve itself constantly, with the help of creativity and imagination.

Core values determine the company's perception and strategy formulation, and ensure consistency in implementation. If values are filled in like this, the company will develop a deep-rooted mentality which can be passed on to all employees. It will be made clear to employees what the company's core values are, what strategy will be implemented, and what the company ultimately wishes to achieve. The human resource policy will often be focused on training managers who can deepen the values and philosophy and spread them through the organization. The whole process of strategic planning is tuned to the company's raison d'être. In the course of strategic reorientation, many companies come to the shocking conclusion that there are too many people in the organization (hidden unemployment); they also discover that the company needs different qualities to ensure its continuity. These qualities have to be found in the objectives, strategy, implementation, and structure of the organization. Many companies unconsciously act this way, others deliberately create a specific structure, and many organizations are totally unaware of the problem.

In the end, the process of defense has to be fluent; nowadays we no longer have the time to correct things. Doubt in taking over the attack can eventually result in damage to one's own organization.

We can see the same thing in the strategic planning process. In many companies, this process and its implementation still take too long. In the Corporate Aikido strategy the process of perception, evaluation, and (re)action is almost one fluent movement. This is also the right approach for strategic policymaking. Usually the strategy developed on the basis of information on the market and the competition is implemented the following year. This is rather like sending the *Pathfinder* to the planet Mars. By the time Houston detects that the Pathfinder is not functioning properly and will cease to operate, this has already taken place. The time gap between the actual event and the interpretation of the data is too big. In a society which moves exponentially faster each day as a result of new information technology, it is important to establish your vision of the environment and the events in it as quickly and regularly as possible. Again, information technology offers the solution here. Information requirements should be defined clearly and explicitly. What is the external environment and from which areas could unforeseen events come? The American retailer Wal-Mart has made it possible to react very quickly to changing patterns in buying. Thanks to an excellent information system, the head office can access the sales results of all the individual stores and distribution centers very soon after closing time. Wal-Mart adapts its assortment policy to this information and supplies its stores right away. Thus, the time factor serves the market and it leads to an advantage over the competition which is known and recognized by the market itself.

A calm and collected way of anticipating and reacting is best in the long run and leads to a balance in the organization. If the defensive process is not right, the perception, interpretation, and evaluation will be wrong, and the defense will not have the desired effect. To avoid this the organization has to be alert so that it can react decisively to each unexpected attack. This demands openness to different events, a good monitoring and navigation system in the organization, and a concentration of energy, of *ki*.

In the prisoner's dilemma (Part 1) we have already discussed briefly perception and the evaluation of the information reaching us. In Fig. 24 you can see that besides perception, the focus of human behavior is also a driving force behind the proper implemen-

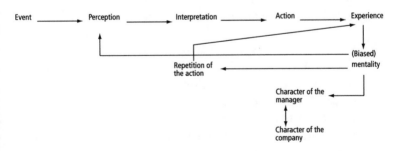

• Figure 24. Perception and attitude of the company.

tation of the aikido principle. Why do people behave the way they do? What drives them on in implementing a certain strategy or taking certain action?

The things people do come from their own egos, their personal experiences, their thoughts and development, the external environment, the situation and the social environment, and their relations with other people. Behavior is always determined by multiple factors. In addition to its own experiences and perception of the relevant issues, the company's behavior is influenced by its people and by the culture and mentality of the organization. This is increasingly being recognized as important by top management, but many people still cannot grasp it. Rational managers find it difficult to take the human factor and the secrets behind human behavior into account. Other managers focus too much on the human component and build an organization *around* people, instead of with people. The idea of *ki* in aikido, the balance between Spirit, Mind, and Body which eventually results in energy (positive and negative), points to merging the company's mission, strategy, and organization.

Managers' actions are mainly driven by their knowledge. They are always spurred on by something, there is a certain direction in their behavior, and good managers persevere. You are motivated to get rid of unpleasant situations, you want to free yourself from pain and move toward pleasure, you are constantly looking for a certain balance. There are also factors that determine behavior. The leader's style is influenced by this behavior and indirectly by those factors. The personality determines the direction; some managers set more difficult objectives than others and wish to reach another level. There are differences in capacity and orientation toward success. A manager is either an "architect" making a design for the future, or a "maintenance mechanic" working on the present situation. Differences like this determine the orientation and the mentality of the company. Because the organization is a combination of people, the mentality and intrinsic energy of one company differs from that of others. This is the difficult aspect of implementation and mentality in the company. Each organization is unique, and herein lies an important source of competitive strength, capacity for growth, energy, or *ki*.

Besides motivation and behavior there is another dominant element in competitive and entrepreneurial behavior (both in attack and defense): perception.

In aikido perception of the attack is crucial for the anticipation and the defense. Many companies spend too much energy in observing the competitor as the primary motivation for their actions; instead they should be concentrating on their policy and monitoring their strategy and competition in case there is an unprovoked attack. In addition to the physical condition (someone who is tired does not function optimally), the physiological condition of the observer and the characteristics of what is observed (the stimuli) are also important.

The perception is determined by the experience of the manager, his mindset, his expectations of what he will observe—in short, the manager's frame of reference. The perception is formed by a complex string of events, activities, interpretations, and experiences. In Fig. 24 this cycle is illustrated simply.

Let us suppose a competitor attacks your company with a new product which is suspiciously like your most important product. You will regard the way you and your management team perceive this event as the actual truth, whereas it is, in fact, only a second view of that truth. In other words, you and your organization are focused, and this focus results in partial perception. This partial perception can lead to a partial solution. It is very important to remain open to more impulses around this event. As mentioned at the beginning of this book, it is important to learn how to forget. This was illustrated by the half-filled glass. The past is not the same as the future. The event has to be interpreted differently, and has to be accompanied by more information than "just" the enthusiastic report on a visit by a rep. Does the consumer experience your product in the same way as you do? How do business partners react to the introduction and what is their motivation for including or not including it in their assortment? What constitutes the product? There are many more questions like this that have to be answered first in order to get as complete a picture of an event and its implications as possible. Try to see the *real* reality.

Perception is formed by your experience and frame of reference. Your frame of reference determines the perception and your opinion of events and situations. Earlier the use of scenarios to "pre-form" this frame of reference was discussed. Here again we see the positive function of scenario thinking. The perception becomes sharper. A manager with lots of (international) experience of all sorts of events with a serious or less serious impact on the company, will react more calmly to specific threats than a manager with a different frame of reference. And to make things more complicated, the people in your organization will perceive their own reality. The bigger the difference between their experiences and between their positions in the experience curve, the more diverse the reactions can be. An organization with a closely knit group of people, a unity, is rooted more firmly in the market than an organization in which the teams are changed regularly. "Perseverance is beneficial," says Confucius.

Our subconscious is formed by the combination of different experiences from the past. At certain events or upon seeing certain objects or people, we recall all sorts of experiences from the past; eventually these are compressed again in an opinion or interpretation. Our consciousness or "normal" thought processes judge the experiences. If you have worked together with someone in your company before, and your memories of this collaboration are less than positive, you will most probably keep on judging this person negatively. You forget that this person might have gained new experience in the meantime, which may have changed his personality completely. Your subconscious does not give you the freedom and space to change your opinion. On the contrary, in seeing this person you are still in the same physical condition as before. From the subconscious your mind leads your body to a similar state of consciousness. It is the same the other way around. If, after 10 years, you meet someone again that you liked very much before, you will get that same pleasant feeling again. If you want to build up the right consciousness, you will have to store the right data in your subconscious mind. Many people think the subconscious cannot be changed at all. This is not true. The subconscious can be changed, but not from one day to the next. And because most people are impatient to correct their preconceived opinion, they will not notice small improvements. They finally stop trying and say they cannot change. If you really want it to, and try for a longer period, your subconscious will change.

In marketing we can see the same in positioning. If a certain product or company with a certain position is introduced, the collective experiences with this product or company will influence the subconscious and the frame of reference of the market. Consistent and consequent education of the market in that position will ensure that the product, the brand, the company, and the world that the brand represents will be rooted firmly in the target group.

In the Netherlands, for example, Douwe Egberts coffee, a brand of Sara Lee Corporation, represents a specific world of experience for the coffee drinker ("And then, there is coffee..."). Starbucks represents the norm for coffee in the United States. The brand is carved in the consumers' mind. In many countries Heineken stands for premium beer, "the best of the best." Hotel guests at Four Seasons have the same fine experience in all countries of the world. American Express, Benetton, Calvin Klein, and Caterpillar are all brand names with positions that represent different worlds of experience for their customers. A good experience is recalled years later, and the same is true of a bad experience. For this reason it takes a lot of money, time, energy, and effort to change market positioning. "The first cut is the deepest" and "you never get a second chance to make a first impression" are relevant phrases that hit the nail on the head here because this is exactly how the subconscious of your target group works.

"Threatening" is a subjective perception. What is considered threatening by one manager may be no problem for another. Experience and the frame of reference form part of what we call "culture." Culture has been defined most clearly as the company's lifestyle. In an organization there are norms and values. These values influence the actions of the organization and its people. It is important to communicate the values of your company clearly and to know the values of your people. By making sure your values are unanimously accepted, your company will become more solid. After this, the different values have to be placed in the right order of priority. This order of priority directs the organization's actions.

Hamel and Prahalad (1994) pointed out the importance of the strategic intention. This is actually the primary driving force behind the company's movements. Underneath this strategic intention lies the priority ladder of the organization's values. They are the positive and negative values that form the engine of the company. If you know these values and communicate them, if these values are accepted, your organization will function as a unit and the external events around it will be perceived more accurately. By observing things more completely, you will also be able to react in the right way. Having the right information important because it can influence the perception. The need for information, or rather, "intelligence," is becoming more crucial every day in forming strategies. There are companies which have formed business intelligence departments with up to 45 people, operating worldwide in important product categories. The interpretation of the information is difficult and challenging. Perceiving it in the right way is, too.

Our subconscious is the product of a chain of conscious experiences. The experiences we have gone through recently are fed by our perceptions and the circumstances around us. In order to change the subconscious, you will have to decide which information should be let through. Useful information should be stored, bad information refused. Everyone is responsible for himself.

Centralization and Coordination

The intrinsic factors are directed at the mentality and attitude of managers and their organizations in starting the defense and controlling the attack. By controlling I do not mean cutting out or destroying the competitor, but actually controlling. The external factors of the defense are the organization and the infrastructure offered by the industrial chain. Of these two groups the first, the internal factors, are the most important and difficult. The techniques of the organization and the infrastructure can be sufficiently learned from management literature and from the examples that appear almost daily in specialist journals and newspapers. But improving the perception, being open to viewing the attack from different angles, and concentrating enough to anticipate or react adequately, requires continuous training. It is useless to concentrate only on the external factors of your defense. These are all aimed at the short term. You must also concentrate on the mental component. The organization and the infrastructure have their limits, but the mind is limitless. Every battle begins with thinking; this is the crucial component. "The mind rules the body," says Tohei (1966).

With the internal factors we speak of "centralization." By centralization I mean the perfect balance and combination of the strategy and the interpretation of that strategy in the whole organization. Communication of the strategy and support for it is of vital importance if we want to achieve centralization. Propagating the norms and values, strategic intention, and core ideology of the organization consistently and consequentially makes it easier to achieve centralization. In the West centralization is sometimes translated as "purposiveness" and "knowing what we stand for." For many employees it is important to know the underlying motivation—why a company thinks and acts in a certain way. Centralization is also the coordination of all the strengths of the organization and its people—mental, organizational, and infrastructural—in order to achieve unity. In this case there will be a clear vision and all conceivable scenarios, and you will not be bothered by external events that may eventually be assessed wrongly.

The clarity of the vision has two sides. First of all the organization has to have a complete, holistic view of the external environment; in this way it can be more alert to specific events in that environment. A holistic view means all the company's target groups, such as the government, pressure groups, workers' councils, unions, suppliers, customers, employees, and stockholders. The specific event has a potential influence on the external environment and on one's own organization. This interaction has to be evaluated properly to enable one to react to it afterward.

The centralization and coordination can also be subdivided in a subjective and objective component (Fig. 25).

One has to be open mentally and independent in order to seize control in this way. The reality is perceived differently by each person, because everyone has a unique background. It is important, however, that you remain open to different perceptions and varying opinions. To achieve this, it is

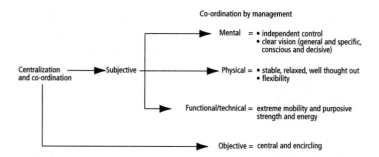

Co-ordination by management

Centralization and co-ordination → Subjective

Mental = • independent control
• clear vision (general and specific, conscious and decisive)

Physical = • stable, relaxed, well thought out
• flexibility

Functional/technical = extreme mobility and purposive strength and energy

Objective = central and encircling

• Figure 25. The centralization and coordination of management.

crucial to have a clear view of the total environment and of the specific event, both consciously and decidedly. The physical condition of the organization has to be stable, balanced, and relaxed, but you should not feel that it is off-guard, sluggish, or arrogant (the "nothing can happen to me" mentality). The functional, technical component is formed by the extreme flexibility that the organization ought to have in order to use its power and energy (ki) purposefully to carry out the defense and seize control. By "objective component" we mean the central idea behind the defense (not destruction) and the extent to which the defensive action "encircles" the attacker or makes the attacker's strengths redundant instead of concentrating on attacking the weaknesses of the competitor.

In discussing the external factors of the defense we shall come back to the basic attitude of the organization, the mentality, the timing and speed of the anticipation, the focus of the defense, and the techniques for neutralizing and controlling the attack. For this basic attitude, I refer to perception and *ki*. In business practice, the timing and speed of the anticipation are decisive for strengthening or losing the competitive position. We will illustrate this with a number of practical examples.

Philips was progressive with its videocassette recording (VCR) 2000 system. Sony introduced its Betamax. Both companies were creating breakthroughs in the video recorder market at the end of the 1970s. A little later JVC entered the market with its VHS system; it passed on the technology for this system to other electronics manufacturers, who were thus able to take advantage of the growth in the video market as well. The first offerer was overtaken and surpassed by JVC and other manufacturers who produced the VHS system. This has nothing to do with the quality of the different systems; we are concerned here only with the passing maneuver of the VHS manufacturers. This phenomenon challenges the traditional economic theory of "decreasing marginal return." The 2000 system and Betamax system were seen at the time as technically superior; but thanks to the marketing approach and the manufacturers that followed, VHS still became the standard.

The QWERTY keyboard (referring to the first six letters at the top left of the keyboard) was introduced in order to slow down the speed of typists; otherwise, the typewriter keys would jam together. In that period, Remington was the market leader, and everybody followed.

When is the market ready for a certain product? In 1984, Sara Lee/DE introduced its decaffeinated coffee in Holland. Earlier attempts to introduce this type of coffee had failed, because the market regarded it as inferior (no caffeine). In 1984, however, the product was relaunched under the name Décafé, in properly balanced packaging; it profited from the health trend which had blown over from the United States.

In 1977, Promech Sorting Systems, an automatized sorting systems company which was taken over in 1997 by the Ro-Group, launched its first sorting system for the distribution of clothing from distribution centers. This was an innovative product at that time. Even so, it took a few years before the company really broke through and its systems were properly appreciated. By 1997, the company had grown into one of the most important niche players in its market. Its systems are used by companies in the United States, Europe, and even Japan.

The fax technology was already operational during World War I, but the actual device was introduced and commercialized only in the 1980s.

Ki, the Life Force of the Company

Unfortunately, enough it is difficult to find the right words to describe *ki* in concrete terms. Western words especially are too limited. In management thinking *ki* can best be translated as the emergence of Spirit, Mind, and Body of the company, enclosing all the unique experiences, norms, and values that ensure the distinctive competence experienced only by those who are part of the company. Your *ki* will be fully unleashed by aligning your personal mission in life, your mind (strategy), and your body. A captain of industry once said that it would be better to speak of "hidden treasures." The *ki* in aikido stands for energy, for breathing power, and the breathing control during a defense. By breathing correctly the defender can lead, neutralize, and control the attack with little or no loss of strength. Gaining control of the situation is the life force of the company, which both spiritually and practically sticks to the principle Winning without Fighting. The way to this result is one of learning and growing. Part 3 will provide some guidelines.

Part 3

Do

The Way There

IT WOULD BE NICE IF THERE WERE A BOOK THAT COULD give answers to all the situations and potential problems of a company. Sadly, such a book does not exist. Actually, it is just as well. In a Corporate Aikido strategy and in applying aikido as a metaphor for a different type of management thinking, you should proceed from your own inner strengths. Trusting yourself and your organization and creating the right infrastructure in life to develop this strength, are the most important starting points for success and growth. Very often decisions are avoided because making them leads to insecurity. And very often decisions are avoided because they imply that one has to *choose*. Still it is important to reduce the risk factor in the decision as much as possible by acquiring the right information quickly, developing scenarios, and having the mindset for anticipation and self-confidence. Great leaders like Turner, Heineken, Hayek, and Dell had and still have such a mindset. Their perseverance and iron will enabled them to take on the challenge.

You will have to be your own student and teacher simultaneously. Experience is the best teacher.

Corporate Aikido is a philosophy based on one of the most difficult martial arts, which uses the principles of "balance and universal life force" and strives for further perfection. With the help of this philosophy, your organization can use its own inner strength to follow the way toward the balance between strategy and implementation, toward its life force. Utilizing core values is difficult, but by no means impossible. Taking over the energy of the opponent, leading and neutralizing the attack will give you control over the situation. Controlling the situation has nothing to do with power, but with creating the infrastructure and possibility to develop further and perfect oneself.

This part will deal first with the possibility of controlling the company (situation). How can you become a "chain *sensei*"? How do you create the space to grow further? Afterward I will provide a few ideas which can serve as a tool for managers in determining their directions and applying the aikido principles.

Chain *Sensei*

If we visualize the possibilities for realizing a distinctive competence with the help of the two value circles (Part 1) and then study the elements on which the market can base its preference for our product or service (Part 2), we will discover that the power to achieve a unique position lies in everything the company does. In the yin-yang figure we talked about a company and its subsequent links in the chain, and saw that they carried out two processes—a demand-generating process and a process which includes all activities that fulfill the demand. The demand-generating process was eventually organized in such a way that it could satisfy to the fullest extent the specific preferences and demands of the market. The demand-fulfilling process was aimed at realizing this in the most effective and efficient way. "Dedication" and "synergy" are opposed and between them is a field of tension that tries to reach a balance.

The company that can create a balance between the dedication of the demand-generating processes and the synergy in the demand-fulfilling processes will become an important force in the market in relation to its competitors. The company that can maintain this balance throughout the whole chain will gain control over the chain and create the infrastructure which allows further growth. My concept of the value circles and the yin-yang principle have been applied many times. In 1997 the concept was utilized to the full during a complex project in China, where it gave direction to top business people from different countries. The results were significant: insight into the new degrees of freedom, cost reductions, different infrastructures, and a concrete migration path for the implementation.

With well-trained process steering, cost reductions can be realized; these savings can then be reinvested in growth. The chain *sensei* is the company which can optimally combine dedication with synergy, and thus direct the chain. Chain *senseis* mobilize their inner strength by optimally adjusting the value circles and the ability to organize the processes in such a way that an unprovoked attack can be controlled.

By striving for the position of chain *sensei*, the company will eventually be able to offer the customers in the market a lower total price for the activities in the business system. Figure 26 (page 139) displays this schematically. The left column represents the product of the competitor and the corresponding price. Absolutely speaking, this price (the marked area) is lower than the price for the product of our company in the example. But because our company is a chain *sensei*, it is able eventually to lower the total costs for the customer by cutting total production time and improving customer and advisory services. This added value reduces the costs in the customer's business system. The difference between the total price if the customer purchases the product from the competitor and the price if it is purchased from the company in the example is called "user economics." These are the economic advantages for the customer.

User economics are determined not only by the costs of the product or service bought by the customer, but by the integral cost consequences which use of the product has in the chain of the purchaser. For example, an ingredient for making bread can be more expensive from some suppliers than from others. If the purchase is based on price, the cheapest ingredient will be chosen. But if the more expensive ingredient leads in the baking to a shorter total production time and better-quality bread, the extra price will be more than proportionately recompensed. The integral costs are reduced. In this case the focus on the chain costs or process costs is more relevant than the price of the ingredient. The intrinsic value of the ingredient is higher than its nominal value.

Another example is that of a provider of logistic services. The services of a provider who not only transports a document from A to B as quickly as possible, but also occupies himself with information technology and organizing the logistic process, may be more expensive in relation to the current transport costs or in comparison with the competition. But the total costs in the logistic circle, including all the client's

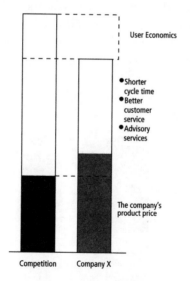

- Figure 26. "User economics" through a balance in the business system and the chain.

processes organized around it, can be significantly lowered. In this way the costs in the processes and in the chain are reduced, and the customer service and market responsiveness for the customer using these logistic services can increase. Thus this client is helped to lower his costs in the business system and reserve more marginal profit for investment in growth or partly pass on the difference to his own customers. In the current situation, and in the new situation, his delivered price is also lowered by the collaboration with the provider of logistic services. This change is illustrated in Fig. 27.

A product or service that is on the market will eventually determine the values and the quality norm. We could say that the market is educated. A frame of reference is created. The way to realizing progress can also be found by redefining the function of a product with the help of user economics.

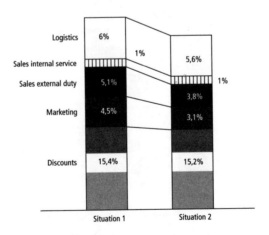

- Figure 27. "Delivered price."

Polaroid developed a different way of looking at user economics, without considering the price. Polaroid built up its reputation by introducing the instant photo. While Kodak was concentrating on new technical characteristics for film and cameras, Polaroid chose a completely different path. It first investigated the activities involved in the processes of buying, use, and development and then concentrated on shortening the total production time. Developing photos took the most time and was experienced by the customers as "waiting too long" for the end result. Polaroid redefined the user economics and thus appealed to a large group of customers.

There is also a third element that can be realized through the chain *sensei* philosophy. By using the provider of logistic services as a supplier for its processes—in other words by farming out their logistic processes and customer service—this company changes the infrastructure of its chain. The company in this example has a fundamental distinction in the market. It reduces the costs of its own processes and business system, the "delivered price" drops, and the infrastructure is used better so that the customer service performance can be strongly improved. If this improvement involves those elements that customers consider important or view critically, the company will be preferred above the other players in the market. In this way it becomes a chain *sensei*, directing the market.

Figure 28 contains an example of a less traditional infrastructure, one without intermediate links. Dell Company changed the infrastructure by marketing their PCs via direct selling.

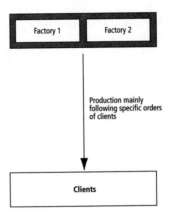

- Figure 28. Changing the existing infrastructure.

The three elements—user economics, delivered price, and infrastructure—have been described here as three separate areas in which distinctive competence can be attained. It goes without saying that one should try to integrate these three areas.

Being Proactive in Using the Value Circles Gives Control

In Corporate Aikido there is no question of "winning" against the competitor; the focus is on winning against yourself. Continuous improvement leads to balance and harmony between strategy and implementation, between the organization and its people; it leads to the universal life force. This is the real distinctive competence. The following guidelines will create space for achieving this in strategic policymaking:

- Apply the Spirit, Mind, and Body concept to your organization.

- Find an answer to the question, What makes my industry tick?

- Integrate the value circles in your strategy.

- Create a balance between demand-generating and demand-fulfilling processes.

- Be aware of user economics, delivered price, and infrastructure.

- Be proactive, like a chain *sensei*.

Linkages and Leverages

What are the possible future results? Industrial chains change in composition. First of all the business systems of individual companies become connected with each other. If you divide activities into demand-generating and demand-fulfilling activities, you can decide to farm out activities that can be carried out better by other companies. This may lead to a rearrangement of functionalities. In this way different companies (direct or indirect competitors, independent companies) can become allies, and "leverage" can be created which can increase the growth potential of the collaborating companies. Because of this collaboration the market results of the companies can be improved and the total costs can be reduced or the added value increased. The added value for the companies and for the market will become significantly higher. Link up business systems in order to create leverage for growth. Companies who are aware of this are able to anticipate this development.

During discussions with senior executives of different companies I drew a comparison with the Rubik's Cube. Earth could be illustrated as a Rubik's Ball, a ball with colors which becomes a three-dimensional puzzle if it is turned. I compared the countries of the world with this Rubik's Ball. Like countries, companies also specialize in front-office and back-office activities, so the world will also be turned around and its color arrangement will be changed. Companies farm out their administrative processes to other financial companies or to countries where the work can be done using relatively cheap labor. Because of developments in information technology, for example, the Internet, the world is now the playing field, and the physical location of a company hardly matters any longer. Publishing houses can use authors from all over the world. Editing can be done in Malaysia, lithography in Italy, and printing in Portugal. Call centers in Houston handle the customer service of financial organizations all over the world. The chain shifts. Linkages and leverages change companies. The composition of industries will change. Due to information technology, countries will gain new comparative advantages, thus economies will alter. This is schematically displayed in Fig. 29.

The value circles, the three areas for creating distinctive competence in the chain and becoming a chain *sensei,* come together in a practical example which is in perfect line with the basic principles of Corporate Aikido. To preserve confidentiality the name of the company and some other specific details have been left out, without diminishing the value of the example.

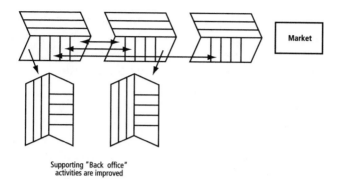

Supporting "Back office"
activities are improved

- Figure 29. Linkages and leverages in the industrial chain will change industries.

A prepublishing company . . . in Europe discovered that the markets in which it had rooted itself were liable to heavy restructuring, price competition, and fragmentation of resources. As a result, turnovers decreased and on average there was not enough turnover per client. Furthermore the profitability of the company was put under pressure; the added value of the products and services was valued in the market, but the market was not willing to pay a supplementary price for it. In recent years different small companies have been bought in order to extend the package of products and services and to profit from new technologies in the prepublishing market. Unnoticed, the company became more complex. Because there were many smaller companies, each with a regional market area, the company no longer fitted in fully with the changing market, where players and customers were becoming bigger. The prepublishing company was able to serve the market well via its individual organizations, but the bigger organizational structure and the positioning hindered full utilization of the market potential. The company fell behind in growth in relation to its potential, and its core values were carried insufficiently in the bloodstream of the organization.

Top management decided to obtain a full picture of the external environment in all its facets and tried to discover different trends and developments which might lead to an unprovoked attack. In addition, the internal resources were evaluated, and the company's basic philosophy and core values were reinvestigated. During this exploration, the price-competitive actions of the biggest "colleague" in the branch were studied as well. Management decided to keep up the quality and avoided price competition by offering a differentiated package of products and services. Because of growth in the past, the costs of the company were no longer in balance. A cost-reduction program was set up, aimed at more efficiency and effectiveness in the activities and processes of the company and its daughter organizations.

Instead of fragmentation of the resources, the company decided to create a new organizational structure in which suboffices were set up from the head office. The individual companies, which previously had all offered part of the prepublishing products and services, were transformed into full satellites, offering the group's whole range of products and services. Internal linkages and leverages were formed which allowed the whole to be more than the sum of the individual parts. As a result, the company was able to supply a bigger market with a different client structure. It was able to fulfill simultaneously the requirements of relatively small buyers and the complex demands of more complex buyers. With the latter group, the company tried to significantly reduce costs in the business system of the clients via a kind of comakership, first by functioning as a junction, and second by taking over activities that could be handled cheaper by the prepublishing firm. By this we do not mean "cheaper than the competition" but cheaper than the buyer. A significant reduction of the costs of the consumer was achieved. Thanks to this relationship, the user economics became fully transparent. The costs in the business system of the buyer were reduced and the results improved. The enormous amount of knowledge, experience, and expertise of this company showed that its inner strength was in the totality of the individual parts. The company managed to create linkages and leverages with its biggest clients and took over complete activities and their coordination. Without troubling itself directly about the competition, the company followed its own course—a course formulated after a fundamental study of the external environment and of the potential events which could have influenced the company positively or negatively. The company led the price competition in the market and neutralized competitors by offering important clients a complete range of products and services. Eventually it controlled the most important market rules and became active in developing new technologies. It focused on its own inner strengths instead of on the weaker points of the competition. Furthermore, the strengths of the competition were made redundant.

This example holds an important key. The key to becoming a chain *sensei* is in creating linkages and leverages (Pino 1994). In this way a win-win situation is created with the buyer. Both parties benefit more than in a situation without linkages and leverages. An idea is to apply this win-win approach to your suppliers as well, or even with other companies with which you can achieve something you could not have achieved otherwise (entering a new market, for instance). Earlier we discussed collaboration with a company that could be your indirect competitor. Linkages and leverages with your market colleague can lead to convergence instead of competition.

The Discipline

A real, clear-cut recipe for Corporate Aikido does not exist. In any event, this would not fit in with the versatility and depth of the martial art. But there are a few guidelines which may offer some support in the thinking process so that the situation can be improved to offer still better opportunities. Experience shows that practicing this martial art yourself reveals the guidelines and principles; this is helpful for the correct application and for discipline in daily life and business. I have tried to filter out the most important guidelines, which can help the company and its employees to take a step in the right direction.

Formulate the Mission and Core Values and Make Decisions

If managers are asked about their goals, they seldom have an answer. If goals have been formulated at all, they are usually extrapolated from the past. Research shows that managers spend very little time on real strategic thinking. Of the 40 percent devoted to studying the external environment, about 30 percent is spent thinking about how the world might look in three, four, five, or more years' time. Then 20 percent of this time is spent on developing a collective view of the future. If we multiply these percentages it turns out that about 2.4 percent of a manager's time is spent on forming a *company vision of the future* (Hamel and Prahalad 1994). In Corporate Aikido a clear view of the environment and the potential events form a crucial basis for the strategy formulation. In addition, the core values of the company and its goals are decisive for the direction the company takes. Decisions and actions, however, must set it in motion. The vision of the environment and a deeper insight into the expectations of the client is very important. After you have obtained a clear view of this, you will be able to define your goals and attempt to become an initiator in serving the market in the best way possible.

Howard Schultz traveled to Italy in 1983 and was incredibly impressed and inspired by the role of coffee in the Italian culture that he decided to bring this concept to the United States and change the U.S. coffee culture. He introduced a premium cup of coffee and a stylish, romantic place to enjoy it. Starbucks was born to become a company that changed the paradigm.

One of the core values of British Airways is the "delight the customer" approach. British Airways defines its product in terms of an experience for the traveler. It defines its services in terms of an experience for the client.

British Airways is aimed at the experience of the consumer. The basis, transportation from A to B, is the same; in general the service and meals are similar; most airlines have a frequent-flyer program, and all flight attendants are equally friendly. British Airways has a special approach for analyzing and understanding the total experience of the consumer. It defines the so-called value-driven needs. By carrying out a thorough and very detailed survey, it obtained insight into the activities as they were experienced by travelers in different segments (business, recreation); by testing proposals it also gained insight into latent needs whose fulfillment would be much appreciated. BA saw that the whole is more than the sum of the parts and that each detail contributes to the total experience.

When British Airways learned from its research that intercontinental travelers did not feel well, they organized a "well-being" program that helped the traveler recover from the journey. The meals were adapted and a video program showed suggestions for simple physical exercises. First-class passengers were offered the chance to dine in a special first-class lounge at the airport, and after dinner they could get pajamas on board the aircraft. On arrival at Heathrow these passengers can make use of "arrival lounges," where they can shower, have their clothes dry-cleaned, have breakfast, and work out. More than 200 intercontinental passengers use this service daily. BA's competitors copy this approach, but the target group knows that British Airways was first with the idea. BA is not frightened by this imitation. Management regards the organization as a holistic system, in which all activities and their purposes are tuned to each other; it trains its employees with this in mind. It strives to completely fulfill the customer's needs, both manifest or implicit. This goal is permanent; furthermore British Airways is always busy studying what the market and the company will look like in 10 to 15 years in order to protect its core values.

Too many managers still do not know the answer if they are asked what their company would look like in 10 or 15 years and where they would be by then. According to them, everything changes so quickly, there is chaos and no use in planning anyway. In this way a kind of company inertia comes into being. What will the company do today to create a new tomorrow that will significantly contribute to the company? Usually the goals of the company are not ambitious enough to generate the energy required for realizing them. Strategic ambition is important and serves as an economic motor for the organization. The goals have to be formulated for different areas:

1. Goals for the company's raison d'être

2. Goals in terms of progress (growth, innovations, improvements)

3. Economic goals (turnover, profit, cost level)

4. Social goals (employees, human resource policy)

An objective cannot function as a motor if no decisions are made. It is important not to postpone decisions. A decision means action, action means result, result means experience, experience means growth, and growth implies better decision making. The future of the company is determined by its core values and the decisions you make. These decisions are fully communicated and deepened inside the organization. In practice it turns out that most people change their strategy completely when a certain decision does not work, instead of learning from the experience and readjusting the action. By implementing the strategy gradually and holding on to the company's core values, the company will grow at the right pace. I call this "bonsai management," the way toward gradual and controlled growth. Information has to be as accurate and complete as possible, in order to make the right decision or take steps. Information is the energy that should make one act. The decisions that have to be taken are in three different areas:

1. Decisions to determine which core values will become decisive for the company (i.e., contributes to its mission)

2. Decisions to determine the direction of the company

3. Decisions on which actions will make the company grow (mentality and in scope, profitability)

Starbucks defined its growth goals for the coming years, resulting in more than 2,000 stores in the year 2000. The company wants to open more stores in the Pacific Rim, will expand in other channels (supermarkets), will stretch its brand by innovations relevant to coffee (for example, as an ingredient for beer), and will grow by using alliances with other companies (Pepsi, Intel, Breyer's ice cream). Growth without losing its core values, its mission.

It is not a problem that the decisions and actions will not always lead to easy paths. By swimming upstream you will overcome disappointments and grow as a person. We have already mentioned that there is no such thing as a good or bad result; there is only the result. Companies usually cling to the means for obtaining results instead of holding on to decisions.

The company's core values and the organization form an important foundation for its decisions and actions. In practice, these core values have to be identified, formulated, communicated, and consistently implemented. The people inside the organization have to feel committed and positive in implementing these core values. People want go from pain to pleasure. If the organization can agree with the core values and if the people realize and accept what the company stands for, implementing the strategy which embraces these values will not be very difficult. The core values, goals, and strategies are very important. If a company does not have these, the environment will force it to choose. In that case the environment takes over the steering wheel, instead of the company functioning as an initiator of new developments that influence or even control the external environment.

In order to take the initiative eventually, many companies wait for the influence of the external environment and especially the competition. You become a passive object instead of a leading subject.

Manage the Perception

We have already indicated that perception and the filtering of reality is decisive for the company's actions and strategy. Usually it is not the events that determine our strategies and actions, but the perception of those events. This perception is itself steered by our earlier experiences and our frame of reference, our generalizations. After that we look to see if an event could have a negative or positive impact on the company, the product, the brand, etc. What is the risk of an event? What is the perceived risk of the action we want to take?

Once accepted perceptions and experiences become a vast system for our actions. The mentality becomes the driving force behind our actions. Here lies the key to progress. The company moves forward by enlarging the frame of reference. In management literature there is sometimes talk of "expedition marketing" (Hamel and Prahalad 1994). In fully testing new products or services on all their ins and outs, there is always the danger of blocking the new development ("paralysis by analysis"). By learning from new developments and experiences one is able to enlarge the frame of reference. Since this is important for the perception of the environment and the potential events in it, the kind of mentality which says "if you don't make mistakes you don't make anything" is needed. This implies that a biased mentality also determines the future of the company, if you hang on to it too much.

Things can also move in the other direction. I don't mean the company's core values, but more that a certain strategy of reaction from the past is the answer to an unexpected and unprovoked attack here and now. Believing firmly in something means that you are sure of it, and this feeling of security leads to a corresponding reaction. The past is not the same as the future, however. The environment, the other players in the market, your own company—everything has changed in relation to the past; better still, you are constantly changing. At the very the moment you read this, you are already changing in some respect.

The extent to which this change is permanent depends on the extent to which outside events take place and the extent to which you undergo experiences. New events only influence our perception only if we are open to them and keep on asking ourselves if the current reactions are still valid. In doing this, you have to strive for continuous improvement and to seek out new possibilities.

Managing the perception and enlarging the frame of reference can best be done gradually. Each experience builds up the perception and the corresponding interpretation. If you try to realize small improvements in the short term in implementing the strategy, you will update the organization on this and send out a signal that the strategy being used is working. Thus, a flywheel is created: once the wheel is turning, it does not take much effort to make it turn faster.

Sometimes a certain perception becomes rusted in the organization—a biased point of view which blocks all kinds of decisions, actions, or events. In these organizations inertia has struck. There is the company, for example, which is convinced that it is the underdog in the market in which it operates. Everything is implemented by the organization with a kind of flatness and the underlying idea that it will not work anyway (a negative *ki*)—this in spite of the fact that this company may have many degrees of strategic freedom in managing complexity, its broad assortment (the only player with such a broad and deep assortment), and a highly respected mother company. A strong will to change is required in order to make a long-term breakthrough in such an organization. If you are aware that something must change and that the organization itself has to change, because the environment never really will, you are already on the right track. Next the organization must truly believe that it *can* change. The self-sabotaging behavior must be changed.

Focus

The example of the prepublishing company, in which each of the companies used to be separately responsible for marketing their own assortment of services, pointed out that success in the market depends on concentrating your resources. At my seminars I sometimes use a metaphor, in which I throw six Ping-Pong balls at one person at once. Nearly always, the person is focused on catching all the balls, but in the end he catches none. He concentrates on catching the balls, but is confronted with too many impulses at one time. If I then throw the six balls one by one at the same person or at six different persons, they are all caught. It does not work to ask one person to do six different things. Either only one task will be carried out correctly or they will all be handled in an average manner.

In aikido focus also determines the action. You have to have a holistic view and be able to survey the whole field, as far as the eye reaches. You can try this by looking straight ahead and registering how far you can see. In this way you are able to concentrate and to observe every movement in the area and react to it; this is possible because you are focused on 180 degrees instead of on a specific point. With a circular movement you can even cover 360 degrees.

In business this focus is also essential. The company has to be focused on the total environment, including all those concerned. To achieve this you require a well-oiled intelligence department. In addition to this, the manager should be focused on the potential events that could have positive or negative implications for the company.

Managers should also try to focus on the company's core values and their consistent implementation. In the Honda case we showed that its encircling strategy toward Harley Davidson was not only creative but also consistent. Nicolas Hayek of Swatch was and is focused on the values of the company, and this was what enabled the Swiss company rise from the ashes like a phoenix. Starbucks is completely "aligned" and focused.

Managers should focus on resources. Because most companies want to do everything at the same time, they turn out to be *senseis* in mediocrity. The company's resources are scattered, and eventually nothing finds resonance in the market. In positioning brands (products, services, retail formulas) companies too often want to be all things to all people. Choices are avoided, and because of this the market does not clearly experience what is being offered by the company.

Finally, managers should focus on the result. After all, the result forms the experience, which in turn forms the perception and the focus on the environment and will potentially influence events. The circle is complete. The five different focus areas are illustrated in Fig. 30.

Ki

A lot has already been written on *ki*, because this is a very important part of aikido. *Ki* is an ancient principle which forms the basis of East Asian philosophies and religions. The actual manifestation of *ki* is different for each person and depends

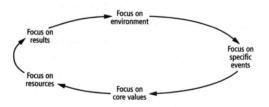

- Figure 30. The company's focus.

on their attitude, frame of reference, ambition, experiences, and background. No two people are alike and the same is true for companies. This is a truth beyond any doubt. The inner energy of the people in the organization determines the character of the company. Moreover, the spirit of the company, its mission, attracts people. In this respect the style of the leader is very influential. An important condition is that the leader communicates the mission and the strategy of the company and creates the infrastructure to utilize and execute the strategy. In Corporate Aikido the *ki* is the fusion of the mission (Spirit), the strategy and culture (Mind), and the organization and the use of the infrastructure (Body). Complete, fluent adjustment determines the activation of *ki*. It is the energy inside the company. In aikido special attention is given to experiencing and controlling *ki*, whereby all defenses are characterized by circular movements.

During my aikido training I learned that the movement must come from the center. This center lies more or less directly below the navel. According to aikido, this is the spot from which the *ki*, or energy, emanates. It is the point of balance and center of gravity. The swing of the hips from this point gives strength. Golfers experience this too; the distance and precision comes from a relaxed position, the balance and swing of the hips. In aikido the energy is led from this point to the point where the defense is started.

In business, *ki* can be found in the middle management level where a balance is required between the strategy (top down) on the one hand and the implementation and market information (bottom up) on the other. If the *ki* has to be used in a defense, the resources flow to a point where the attack can be controlled, ethically directed, and aimed at making the strengths of the opponent redundant. The energy of the company will be concentrated on the area where it will have to take over and neutralize the attack—always with an intention which seems to presume that everything has already happened.

In Conclusion

Aikido is also called the discipline of coordination, the coordination of Spirit, Mind, and Body. Leading the attack via circular movements, taking over the energy, neutralizing the strength of the opponent, and controlling the situation, all without force or tension. Aikido proves that there is no winning or losing, that you can perceive reality with an open mind and can anticipate unexpected events. Even before the attack is physically started, the *aikido-ka* can take action and seize control. The purposive attacking or anticipation force, together with a balance of strategy and resources and the mentality of your organization, will enable you to control the situation and to determine your own future.

Aikido is a martial art characterized by these features and it selects its practitioners. It is a discipline of coordination so versatile and difficult that this aspect forms its own basic principle—striving constantly for perfection. In today's business world this search for perfection is required as the driving force to move forward and to add value. Increasing your value requires the will to grow—growing through inner strength and with the will to learn and to contribute to prosperity, to value. Value for yourself, for the company, for your colleagues, and last but not least, for your customers. This is a challenge for managers—not just a challenge for you personally but also for your company. Just reading this book is not enough. You will have to understand the principles, apply them and be willing to learn from them. This book can help you to achieve this. Aikido is too versatile, however, for it to be described completely in one book. I advise the reader to take up this book frequently and to reread certain parts. In this way you will gain new insights in the course of time. Those new ideas are your merits and they will fit in with the motivation of Morihei Ueshiba, the founder of aikido, and with his concept as the way of harmony and balance which strengthens the unity between the spirit, mind, and body, between yourself and others. Or, in terms of *Corporate Aikido*, between the mission, the strategy, and your organization. That is what real *ki*, which contributes to everyone, everywhere, is really about. Your fusion of your personal mission, your personal strategy, and a fit body gives you undeniable inner strength. The alignment of spirit, mind, and body unleashes the potential within your company to neutralize competition and to seize growth continuously.

Recommended Reading

Axelrod, Robert. *The Evolution of Cooperation.* New York: Basic Books, 1984.

Collins, James C., and Jerry I. Porras. *Built to Last: Successful Habits of Visionary Companies.* London: Random House, 1995.

Dang, Tri Thoung. *Beyond the Known.* Tokyo, 1993.

D'Aveni, Richard. *Hypercompetition: Managing the Dynamics of Strategic Maneuvering.* New York: The Free Press, 1994.

De Geus, Arie. *The Living Company: Habits for Survival in a Turbulent Environment.* Cambridge, Mass.: Harvard Business School Press, 1997.

Hamel, Gary, and C. K. Prahalad. *Competing for the Future: Breakthrough Strategies for Seizing Control of Your Industry and Creating the Markets of Tomorrow.* Cambridge Mass.: Harvard Business School Press, 1994.

Heider, John. *Tao of Leadership.* New York: Bantam New Age Books, 1985.

Hammer, Michael, and James Champy. *Reengineering the Corporation: A Manifesto for Business Evolution.* New York: HarperBusiness, 1993.

Meyer, Herbert E. *Real-World Intelligence: Organized Information for Executives.* New York: Weidenfeld & Nicolson, 1987.

Pino, Robert. *Strategische Overdenkingen.* Schiedam, The Netherlands: Scriptum, 1994.

Senge, Peter M. *The Fifth Discipline: The Art and Discipline of the Learning Organization.* New York: Doubleday, 1990.

Sun-Tzu. *War and Management.* Singapore: Addison-Wesley, 1991.

"Swatch," *Harvard Business Review,* March-April, 1993.

Tohei, Koichi. *Ki in Daily Life.* Tokyo: K. N. Kenkyukai HQ, 1978.

Tohei, Koichi. *Aikido: The Art of Self-Defense.* Tokyo: 1991.

Ueshiba, Kisshomaru. *The Spirit of Aikido.* Tokyo: Kodansha Int. Ltd., 1984.

Westbrook, A., and O. Ratti. *Aikido and the Dynamic Sphere.* Tokyo: Charles E. Tuttle Company, 1970.

Index

About the Author

Robert Pino has gained many years of business experience at strategic and commercial decision making in national and international management positions at Sara Lee/DE and A. T. Kearney. He has received numerous distinctions in the area of business strategy and he has published a great many articles on marketing and strategy. His business seminars are highly regarded. Robert Pino is the founder, president, and CEO of Robert Pino & Company, strategy consultants, with offices in Chicago, Rotterdam, and Hong Kong. Their clients include a number of the world's largest multinationals and Fortune Global 1,000 companies. He is a consultant and coach to managers of reputable companies in North America, Europe, and the Far East.